Open House

Open House

A Guide to Buying and Selling Hawaii Real Estate

Roy M. Kodani

A Kolowalu Book • University of Hawaii Press • Honolulu

© 1991 University of Hawaii Press
All rights reserved
Printed in the United States of America
91 92 93 94 95 96   5 4 3 2 1

Library of Congress Cataloging-in-Publication Data

Kodani, Roy M., 1939–
Open house : a guide to buying and selling Hawaii real estate /
Roy M. Kodani.
p.   cm. — (A Kolowalu book)
Includes index.
ISBN 0–8248–1318–9
1. Vendors and purchasers—Hawaii.   2. Real estate business—Law
and legislation—Hawaii.   3. Real property—Hawaii.   I. Title.
KFH126.K63   1991
346.96904'37—dc20
[349.6906437]   90–26966
                                                           CIP

University of Hawaii Press books are printed
on acid-free paper to meet the guidelines
for permanence and durability of the Council
on Library Resources

*Chapter opening computer drawings
by Alexandru P. Preiss*

To my mother and father,
Toyoko and Asawo Kodani

With my deepest gratitude
and appreciation

Contents

Acknowledgments   ix

Introduction   xi

1. What Happens in the Typical Purchase of a Home?   1

2. What Is Real Estate?   4

3. What Are the Types of Residential Real Estate?   7

4. Why Retain a Real Estate Broker?   19

5. Should You List Your Property for Sale?   27

6. Should You Hire an Appraiser?   31

7. What Other Professional Assistance Do You Need?   38

8. Who Are the Seller and the Buyer?   42

9. What Are the Essential Elements of a Contract to Purchase and Sell?   55

10. How Should You Finance the Purchase of the Property?   61

11. Do You Have Good Title to Your Property?   75

12. Are There Special Precautions in Acquiring Shoreline Properties?   87

13. What Happens at a Closing?   93

14. In What Tenancy Should the Property Be Held?   100

15. Should You Obtain Title Insurance?   107

16. What Is Recordation?   110

17. What Is Conveyance Tax?   116

18. What Should You Know About Real Property Tax?   119

19. What Are Your Rights When the Other Party Breaks the Contract?   125

20. How Is Land Use Regulated? 129

21. Should You Insure Your Property? 134

22. To Lease or Not to Lease? 138

23. What Are Your Rights When Your Property Is Condemned? 144

24. What Happens When Your Property Is Foreclosed? 147

25. What Happens to Your Property When You Die? 151

Appendix A. Classes of Real Estate 159

Appendix B. Government Offices 165

Appendix C. Sample Forms 169
Deposit Receipt, Offer and Acceptance 170
Seller's Counter Offer 172
Standard DROA Addendum 173
Seller's Real Property Disclosure Statement: Single-Family Residences and Vacant Land 177
Seller's Real Property Disclosure Statement: Condominium Apartment and Townhouse 179

Cases and Statutes Cited 181

Index 183

Acknowledgments

Although a book is the product of its author, the final result contains the contributions of the many individuals who assist the author from the time the idea for the book germinates until publication.

I would be remiss if I neglected to thank everyone who assisted me in making this book a reality. A special mahalo to Michelle Osborn, Susan Sensui, and Anne Klemme. They patiently assisted me by typing many drafts of the manuscript. I express my gratitude to Iris M. Wiley, of the University of Hawaii Press, for her time, effort, and wonderful ideas. Without her, this book would not have been possible. Last but not least to my family, for their support and understanding, my warmest aloha.

Introduction

The three human necessities are food, clothing, and shelter. In Hawaii, as in other parts of the world, the home is the most costly of the three necessities and usually the biggest investment of a lifetime. To protect your home, which is an investment in real estate, it is extremely important to know your rights, duties, and liabilities in acquiring and owning real estate in Hawaii.

Statistics clearly show that the average cost of a home in Hawaii is appreciably higher than on the mainland. The scarcity of available urban and suburban land is one reason for the high cost. Oahu, for example, is a small island to start with, and much of the usable land is owned by the federal, state, or city government or by one of the large estates or corporations. Recent statistics show that 32 percent of Oahu's land is owned by the public sector: the federal government owns about 45 percent, the state government owns 45 percent, and the City and County of Honolulu owns the remaining 10 percent. The availability of privately owned real property for development of homes is further reduced by land use laws and zoning.

Private land owners who wish to develop their lands may be affected by tax laws, financing, and governmental regulations. In fact, highly restrictive land use controls and bureaucratic red tape, which often cause delays in the development of land, are cited as the second reason for the high cost of constructing residences in Hawaii. The third reason is the high cost of development, including labor and materials costs. Yet home ownership in Hawaii has proved to be an excellent investment, because the value of homes has increased significantly over the years. With the information in this book, the homeowner should be better able to protect that investment and in a prudent fashion.

It is my hope that you, the homeowner or home purchaser, will become familiar enough with the legal requirements of home purchase and ownership to ask the right questions at the right time. Unless you are aware of the legal requirements and their consequences, you may not realize the significance or implications of information that is given to you—or withheld from you—as a real estate purchaser or homeowner. In order to buy a home with confidence, you must have *all* the information and if you do not, you should know what questions to ask.

The format of this book is chronological, proceeding from the steps leading to the purchase of a home, the contract to sell and purchase the home, and the process of closing the purchase and sale, to the problems that occur when either the seller or the purchaser refuses to live up to his or her end of the bargain, and, finally, to the rights and responsibilities of a homeowner after the purchase of a home.

Although the basic real estate laws in Hawaii are similar in most respects to those in other states, Hawaii also has some unique laws governing real estate that came about through legislation or through judicial decisions (referred to as *common law*). Every effort has been made to call the readers' attention to those particular laws.

This book is intended to give a bird's-eye view of the real estate laws in Hawaii focusing on residential property. It is intended to be a reference for anyone interested in learning the legal aspects of acquiring and owning real estate in Hawaii. It is by no means intended to give complete, comprehensive, and in-depth coverage of all aspects of the real estate laws. As complicated as the law is, it is

constantly being changed by the state legislature, the county gov-
ernments, the courts, and Congress. With the laws constantly
changing, even during the time between the writing and publication
of this book, it is important to consult an attorney to keep apprised
of the current law or for answers to legal questions.

The complexity of real estate should alert you of the advisability
of consulting with competent professionals and specialists in the
field. Do not substitute this book for a lawyer, certified public
accountant, tax expert, or other professional when the occasion calls
for professional assistance.

1 What Happens in the Typical Purchase of a Home?

This book describes the typical real estate transaction involving the purchase and sale of a home in Hawaii. Although the discussion is certainly applicable to commercial and industrial properties, the main purpose of the book is to assist the seller and buyer of residential property in Hawaii.

The following is a typical case in which a buyer decides to purchase residential property: A couple, let us call them Jon and Ann Homeseekers, are a two-income family with no children renting a one-bedroom apartment in Makiki, Honolulu, Hawaii. They have managed to accumulate some savings and now wish to have a home of their own. How do they go about finding a home to purchase? There are many ways to start. They can check the local newspapers to see what residences are available, or talk to family and friends, or visit homes for sale that have "open houses" for inspection, usually on weekends.

Sooner or later, Jon and Ann learn that it is to their advantage, saving both time and effort, to seek the professional assistance of a real estate broker or salesperson. For Jon and Ann, finding the right broker is no easier than finding the right home. An entire chapter in this book (chapter 4) is devoted to real estate brokers, but, for now, let us say that Jon and Ann ask a broker to assist them. The broker must narrow down the kind of residence they are interested in acquiring (for instance, do they want a single-family dwelling or a condominium?), the price they can afford, and the location where they are interested in living.

For our present purposes, let us assume that with the broker's professional assistance, after looking at several homes, Jon and Ann find a single-family home to their liking in Mililani Town. It is owned by Joe and Mary Seniors, who are both retired and intend to move into a condominium, and they are also represented by a broker. Jon and Ann inspect the home two, three, or even more times to be sure that it is the home they wish to acquire. They are also given a copy of the Seller's Real Property Disclosure Statement, prepared by the sellers and containing information on the sellers' home. The broker representing Jon and Ann then prepares a contract to purchase the residence at a price and on the terms and conditions that he* has discussed with them. The offer is signed by Jon and Ann. The contract, which is called a Deposit Receipt, Offer, and Acceptance (DROA), together with a partial down payment, usually a check, is then presented to the sellers' broker.

If the price or the terms and conditions are not satisfactory to the sellers, a counter-offer prepared by the sellers' broker is presented to Jon and Ann through their broker. Further negotiations may occur, but Jon and Ann finally do accept the changes requested by the sellers in their counter-offer. They indicate their acceptance by signing the counter-offer document. Then, the DROA, the counter-offer, the Seller's Real Property Disclosure Statement, and the down-payment check are delivered to an escrow, essentially a neutral third party whose basic function is to assist in completing the purchase

---

*A writer faces a dilemma. The English language does not contain a one-word equivalent for "he or she," yet it is cumbersome to repeatedly refer to someone as "he or she." Therefore, for the sake of readability, "he" and "she" in this book includes both genders.

and sale of the home. A more detailed explanation of the duties and responsibilities of an escrow are spelled out later in this book.

Thereafter, or as they are negotiating to purchase the home, Jon and Ann may discuss with the loan officer of a bank or a savings and loan institution getting a loan to pay the balance of the purchase price (the amount of the loan will be equal to the purchase price minus the initial down payment and any other cash payment). Most often, the broker assists in finding a lender to make a loan to the buyers at a reasonable interest rate and on terms convenient for the buyers. The big question for Jon and Ann, after taking into consideration their net monthly compensation, is whether they can handle the monthly mortgage payments.

Then, prior to closing, the date set in the DROA, Jon and Ann will sign the loan documents, the closing statement prepared by the escrow, and all the other required documents and forms to purchase the home. In turn, Joe and Mary, as the sellers, sign the deed transferring ownership of the home to Jon and Ann. Usually a day or two after all documents are signed, the escrow will record the documents at the Bureau of Conveyances, a state agency where all real estate documents are recorded. Officially, the day all required documents are recorded is referred to as the *closing*. Immediately after the recordation of the documents, the net sale proceeds are paid over to the sellers, and the buyers receive a copy of the recorded deed.

The case described above is a condensed version of the typical purchase and sale of a residence in Hawaii. It provides a bare bones chronology from the beginning to the end of what happens when residential real estate is purchased, and it contains an oversimplified description of the typical transaction, which is more complicated and involves many more steps before being consummated successfully. It has been presented here to give a general outline of the material in this book. The book starts with some basic information about real estate, and then it will guide you step by step from the time you decide to purchase a home to the closing, when ownership is transferred to you as the buyer. It continues by providing you with information that should be helpful to you as the property owner after the purchase.

2 What Is Real Estate?

The terms *land, realty, real property,* and *real estate* are often used interchangeably and are sometimes thought to be identical in meaning. In many instances, the distinction may not be critical or essential. However, each term has its own technical meaning and legal significance.

Land is more than just that part of the surface of the earth not covered by water. It starts at the center of the earth, passes through the earth's surface, and continues into space. Thus, a land owner has rights to the subsurface and air rights above the surface of the ground. Land also includes all of its natural assets, such as water, minerals, trees, and—on the mainland—oil.

Realty includes land and improvements to the land. Examples of improvements are buildings and structures constructed on the land and other man-made additions to or on the land, such as driveways, sidewalks, curbs, swimming pools, outdoor water sprinkler systems, utilities, and fences.

Real estate refers to realty and the right to own and use it. Hence, your interest in a particular real estate simply refers to your right to own and use that specific land and all the improvements on the land.

Real property signifies the right to own realty. The term is often used to distinguish real estate from personal property.

The distinction between real property and personal property is important, primarily because a real estate transaction may include or exclude personal property. If a sale excludes personal property and you, the buyer, do not understand what personal property is, you may presume that certain items found in the residence are included in the sale. *Personal property* refers to the right and privilege of ownership of intangible as well as physical objects that are movable and not attached to land.

> EXAMPLE: As a prospective buyer, you see a china hutch in the dining room of the residence you decide to purchase. It is large in size but movable. Without question, it is personal property. You assume because of its size that the hutch is to be included as part of the sale of the residence and thus fail to negotiate it as part of the purchase. Ultimately it is not included as part of the sale of the residence, since the hutch is not part of the realty.

> EXAMPLE: A franchise, which is a privilege granted by the owners of a trademark or trade name to another person to sell a product or service under that mark or name, is an example of an intangible right. If you purchase a well-known hamburger restaurant but fail to include the franchise as part of the purchase, you will find yourself owning a hamburger restaurant without the right to use the well-known hamburger trademark or trade name.

Personalty refers to movable objects not attached to land. Such objects are also called *chattels*. Included are such items as cars, furniture, appliances, exercise equipment, and computers.

The distinction between real and personal property is also important because the legal requirements for ownership and the transfer of rights are different. For instance, specific legal provisions need to be stated in a legal instrument (document) called a *deed* when the transfer of interest involves real property. If the transfer were to include personal property, a separate instrument called a *bill of sale* would need to be prepared.

There is yet another category of property, which is classified as *fixtures*. Fixtures are personal property that are attached to land or a building and which the law deems to be a part of the real estate. Examples include elevators and kitchen cabinets.

Generally, when real estate is conveyed (transferred), the fixtures are automatically a part of the real estate that is sold. However, there are certain fixtures that are not deemed to be a part of the real estate. *Trade fixtures* are personal properties owned by a tenant of a rented commercial premises that are attached to the premises for use in the tenant's business: store shelves and restaurant equipment, for instance. Trade fixtures may be removed and taken by the tenant when the lease expires.

When looking at a home that you contemplate purchasing, if you find personal properties in, on, or affixed to the residence, you should inquire whether they are fixtures to be included in the sale. If there is any question in your mind, it should be settled with the seller before you sign the contract and not later, when it is too late. Do not be afraid to ask questions. To avoid future problems, do not assume anything.

> IMPORTANT POINT: A home is real estate. Personal property in the home is generally not included in the sale of the home unless it is considered a fixture.

3 What Are the Types of Residential Real Estate?

The decision to acquire a home of your own is only the first step. The second step is to decide what type of home you wish to own and live in. The residence you live in will be a structure; however, there are different legal consequences depending on what type of residential real estate it is. The following are the better-known types of residential real estate in Hawaii: house and lot, condominium, cooperative apartment (co-op), and subdivision.

House and Lot

The most popular type of residential property is the house and lot. The owner has full ownership of the entire property (the house and the lot) rather than a form of community living that involves sharing ownership. The greatest advantage of owning a house and lot is the complete and total control you, the owner, have over your property. You need not consult with anyone in any decision making.

With regard to when and how much to spend on the maintenance of the dwelling, for instance, you are free to make any and all decisions.

Ownership of a house and lot refers to one residential structure on one parcel of land. The land on which the house is built may be owned either in fee simple (absolute ownership) or as a leasehold, which is generally a long-term lease with a written agreement between the land owner (lessor) and the homeowner (lessee). The terms of residential leases have ranged from fifty-five to sixty years. The use of the land will be governed by the terms of the lease agreement. The acquisition of the residential long-term lease is discussed in chapter 22.

If instead of purchasing a lot with a house, you decide to purchase a vacant lot with the intent to construct a single-family dwelling on it, you or your architect, who is retained to draw the plans for your residence, should first check with the zoning or planning agency of the county in which the lot is located to be sure that the zoning ordinance allows a single-family dwelling to be constructed on the lot. If such a dwelling is permitted, you should then study the local zoning and building requirements, which will affect the height and dimensions of the residence and its setback from the property boundary.

Incidentally, there is another reason for finding out the zoning of the vacant land before purchasing it for the construction of a residence. The real property taxes for the parcel may not be economically feasible for the construction of a single family dwelling.

EXAMPLE: The parcel of land may be zoned "apartment," in which case the real property tax is considerably higher than for a parcel zoned "residential." The higher tax forces many owners of single-family dwellings to sell their properties when zoning is changed from residential to apartment. The increase in real property tax makes it no longer feasible to reside on the apartment-zoned property. The alternative to selling would be for the property owner to construct an apartment building. However, the owner may not wish to do so or may not be able to afford to do so.

A relatively new but growing development is *ohana housing,* which allows a second housing unit on certain residential lots (*ohana* is the Hawaiian word for family). The second unit is considered an accessory dwelling to the first dwelling. In passing the ohana housing legislation in the City and County of Honolulu, the city government recognized the high cost of acquiring real estate and constructing a home in the City and County of Honolulu. To alleviate the housing shortage, ohana housing has been permitted in designated areas where two dwelling units are not ordinarily permitted on one parcel of land. The second dwelling unit may be a separate structure or attached to an existing structure. Each county has maps showing the parcels of land that allow ohana housing.

Prior to applying for a building permit to construct the accessory dwelling, you should precheck the construction plans with the Building Department to determine whether the plans meet the legal requirements for ohana housing. The necessary forms can also be picked up at the Building Department.

REFERENCE: Ohana Housing. Section 6.20, *City and County of Honolulu Land Use Ordinance.*

Condominium

The condominium in Hawaii provides apartment-type residential living that appeals to many because it frees the apartment owner from having to maintain a single-family dwelling and landscape the property, and, in most instances, vacations can be taken with less worry about the security of the home.

As a condominium owner, you enjoy exclusive ownership of your apartment unit, usually as a fee-simple interest, and you retain an undivided percentage interest in the common elements of the condominium project that all apartment owners are entitled to use or have ownership rights in. An undivided percentage interest is your share of the total interest; however, it cannot be separated or segregated from other owners' shares. You maintain your own apartment, and an association of apartment owners (AOAO) consisting of all apartment owners in the building is established and charged with the responsibility of maintaining the common elements of the building. The association raises the funds necessary to maintain the common elements by charging association dues and assessing maintenance fees upon each owner.

The legal document creating the condominium (referred to legally as the condominium property regime) is the Declaration of Condominium Property Regime, which is filed with the Real Estate Commission, an agency connected with the Department of Commerce and Consumer Affairs of the State of Hawaii. Each apartment's common elements and limited common elements (common elements restricted for the use of certain apartments) are enumerated in the declaration.

Common elements means and includes

1. The land included in the condominium project, whether leased or in fee simple;

2. The foundations, columns, girders, beams, supports, main walls, roofs, halls, corridors, lobbies, stairs, stairways, fire escapes, and entrances and exits of the building or buildings;

3. The basements, flat roofs, yards, gardens, recreational facilities, parking areas, and storage spaces;

4. Central and appurtenant installations for services such as power, light, gas, hot and cold water, heating, refrigeration, air conditioning, and incinerators;

5. The elevators, escalators, tanks, pumps, motors, fans, compressors, ducts, and in general all apparatus and installations existing for common use;

6. Facilities designated as common elements in the declaration; and

7. All other parts of the property necessary or convenient for the common elements' maintenance and safety or used as a common element.

An owner's proportionate interest in the common elements must be explicitly stated in the sales information and the conveyance instrument (the legal document transferring interest in real property from one person to another). You, as the buyer, receive a conveyance instrument when you purchase a condominium apartment.

You may also own *limited common elements*. Limited common elements generally adjoin an apartment. They may include carports, lanais, balconies, and entryways.

The condominium statute is a disclosure law, which means that the condominium developer and the first seller of the condominium apartments have the legal duty to furnish all of the information required by law to the buyer of the condominium. The intent of the law is to require the developer and the first seller to provide sufficient information to the interested buyer for the buyer to make an informed decision whether to purchase a condominium apartment. The statute specifies the information that must be furnished to the interested buyer of a condominium in a new project or a conversion (an existing building converted into a condominium). The law requires the developer to furnish the buyer with a preliminary or final public report on the condominium project issued by the Real Estate Commission. The report is not issued until all the required information has been submitted to the Real Estate Commission. Without the report, no condominium can be offered for sale or sold.

The preliminary report is not issued until the Real Estate Commission is satisfied that it adequately discloses all material facts that an interested buyer should consider in purchasing a condominium. Also, the developer or the first seller must provide adequate protection of the purchaser's down payment and other additional payments. For instance, the buyer's down payment must be deposited in a trust account with an escrow, a neutral third party who has no vested interest in the buyer's down payment.

No final public report is issued until the deed or master lease for the land on which the condominium building is located is signed and recorded. The Declaration of Condominium Property Regime and a true copy of the bylaws and floor plans approved by the county officer who issues building permits must also be signed and recorded.

The operation of a condominium project is governed by the bylaws, and no amendment to the bylaws is valid unless the amendment is recorded. In the usual situation, the apartment owners elect officers and directors of the association of apartment owners, and they in turn hire a professional managing agent to handle the operations and maintenance of the condominium on a day-to-day basis. Every managing agent is required to register with the Real Estate Commission.

REFERENCE: Condominium. Chapter 514A, *Hawaii Revised Statutes.*

Cooperative Apartments (Co-op)

The cooperative apartment concept, referred to as a "residential cooperative corporation" under the Hawaii statute, has not really taken off in Hawaii, although in the early 1960s it appeared that it might make inroads on the real estate market.

The co-op owner has an interest in a corporation that owns a multiunit building, like a shareholder of a corporation which in turn owns the building. In a co-op, the owner also has a lease entitling him or her to occupy a unit in the building. The lease is usually referred to as a *proprietary lease,* and the term of the lease is for a set number of years. Therefore, the co-op owner does not legally own the apartment in which he or she lives. It is technically owned by the corporation, which leases the apartment to the co-op owner. The corporate form is generally used because it is a practical way of taking title to a property, electing and controlling officers and directors, and providing for centralized management, while at the same time it protects the individual co-op owners from personal liability for corporate obligations. Thus, whereas a condominium owner has an interest in real estate that he or she can transfer freely to anyone, the co-op owner is the owner of shares of stock in a corporation that are transferable as personal property.

Proprietary leases generally have an initial term of twenty to fifty years and are renewable by the corporation, which is the lessor, and the co-op owner, as the lessee, at the end of the term. The lease rent includes the cost of maintaining the co-op building, insurance, and real property taxes. The rent may escalate when certain conditions occur such as an increase in real property taxes or an increase in the cost of maintaining the co-ops. The costs included in the co-op lease rent are similar to the costs computed in the condominium maintenance fees.

Besides the proprietary lease, which is always present in a co-op, there may also be a land lease, if the land on which the co-op is located has been leased from the land owner. The land lease (also referred to as the ground lease) may require periodic reappraisal of the land in order to determine the new rent for the periods following the initial term. In most instances, the new rent that is renegotiated will be based on an agreed upon percentage of the fair market value of the land set forth in the land lease agreement. If the fair market value cannot be settled, then arbitration occurs in which case appraisers are hired to determine the fair market value of the land.

> EXAMPLE: The land lease may provide that the lease rent will be renegotiated at the end of twenty years and that the new annual rent shall be 7 percent of the fair market value of the land. Thus, if the land value is $1,000,000, then 7 percent of $1,000,000 is $70,000 or $5,833.33 per month. The $5,833.33 is then divided by the number of units in the co-op to determine what each co-op's share of the rent shall be.

Under no circumstances can the proprietary lease be separated from the cooperative stock. Neither can be sold or transferred independently from the other. The stock certificate is the evidence of ownership in the co-op. The proprietary lease sets forth the rights of the co-op owners and the corporation and the legal obligations that exist between them and among the co-op owners. As in the case of the condominium, management is assumed by an elected board of directors and officers who may operate through a managing agent.

The major disadvantage of the co-op is the obligation imposed on the co-op owner to pay a proportionate share of the mortgage payment and real property taxes of the entire co-op project. The condominium owner is liable only for the mortgage on his or her own apartment and a share of the monthly maintenance fees. A co-op owner is dependent on the financial condition of the other owners in the project. If any one of the owners fails to pay his share of the monthly charges, the delinquency could result in a default, and other owners may have to cure the default in order to avoid a foreclosure or lien on the entire project. In a condominium, the default of one apartment owner will not jeopardize the interest of the other owners in the building.

Whereas the single-family dwelling owner or the condominium

owner can refinance his mortgage, the co-op owner is bound by a mortgage covering the entire project and is not able to obtain a pro rata share of the mortgage or a mortgage only for his unit. Hence, the co-op owner is unable to refinance his co-op, as other home owners, for cash, education, or home improvements.

Most co-op leases or bylaws require approval of the prospective buyer by the board of directors before the buyer is allowed to purchase a unit in the co-op. This requirement allows the board of directors the right to pass on a new owner's credit. This approval process is important, because all of the owners have a substantial capital investment in the co-op and a direct interest in the financial stability, character, reputation, and personal conduct of the other owners in the co-op. It is a well-known fact that the more luxurious the co-op, the more difficult the approval process is. Banks hesitate to make loans secured by a cooperative stock and lease without written consent of the board of directors.

In sum, the differences between a condominium and a co-op are

Condominium	*Co-op*
Owner takes direct title in unit.	Owner takes stock ownership in co-op and a lease right to occupy a unit.
Owners vote on a proportionate basis.	Owner has one vote regardless of size of unit.
Each unit is taxed separately.	Owners pay a share of total charges.
Owner is responsible only for the mortgage and tax on his own unit.	Each owner is dependent on the solvency of the entire co-op.

Subdivision

A subdivision is a parcel of land divided into smaller parcels (lots) that are subject to certain controls. The house and lot discussed earlier in this chapter may be a part of a subdivision. A great number of the residential dwellings developed recently in Hawaii are part of a subdivision and fall under strict subdivision and zoning regulations. Each county in the state has its own planning and zoning code, rules and regulations, legal interpretations, and administrative policies.

Subdivision controls have been enacted by the counties to ensure the orderly development of the land set aside for urban use by each county. Regulations concern streets, utilities, public services (fire and police protection), educational facilities, and transportation. The county ordinances place responsibilities on developers for the orderly development of the community.

In most counties, developers are required to apply for subdivision approval of a project. Notice is given the public of a hearing on the application, and after the hearing, the appropriate county department approves or denies the application. If approved, the file plan showing the subdivision lots is recorded with the Bureau of Conveyances, which is the office where all real estate documents are recorded in Hawaii.

In order to compel lot owners to maintain a standard in the use and enjoyment of their lots, the developer of the subdivision records a Declaration of Covenants, Conditions, and Restrictions, which encumbers (places a burden upon) the lots with restrictive covenants (agreements) running with the land for a set number of years. Generally, the declaration restricts and regulates the use and enjoyment of the lots regarding the kind, character, and location of the residential structure and other structures that may be erected on the lots. Because the covenants run with the land, they continue to be applicable even if there is a change of ownership from one person to another.

In Hawaii, restrictions are commonly placed on the height of a dwelling structure, the part of the lot on which a dwelling may be constructed (in order to maintain the view corridor of other property owners), the minimum construction cost of homes, and the presence of farm animals on the property. It is illegal for a covenant to restrain the alienation (transfer) of property on the basis of color, creed, race, or national origin.

The most common form of restrictive covenants is found in the general plan of development covering a tract of land divided into lots. In such a case, the developer inserts the covenants in the deeds of all lots subdivided from the one parcel of land for the benefit of all lot owners. By the establishment of the covenants, the developer indicates to prospective lot buyers the kind of neighborhood environment that is to be created. The purchaser buying a lot with restrictive covenants adopts the general building plan intended by the covenants. Such a purchaser is willing to pay a higher price for his lot, because the restrictions are intended to maintain building standards that will protect the overall neighborhood environment and thereby add value to his property.

Homeowners Association

Owners of detached (freestanding structures) and attached (living units within multi–living unit structures) single-family dwellings who share community facilities usually form homeowners associations in which members own participating shares. Such associations are popular in cluster developments in which open space is promoted as a feature of the project. The homeowners association is usually created to provide common ownership of recreational centers and green areas. As a condition of approving new developments, counties now require developers to form homeowners associations to maintain properties such as parks, streets, and sidewalks, which were previously maintained by the counties.

The association form of community ownership is often preferred over the condominium or co-op form, because the homeowner owns his or her individual home outright with a membership share in the homeowners association. There are no common or limited common elements in a homeowners association. Furthermore, on resale of her property the homeowner has less explanation to give prospective buyers about common responsibilities than would be the case for a condominium or co-op.

Time Sharing

The purchase of a vacation home promoted and sold to a number of owners, each of whom buys a designated time during which he uses the living unit each year, is referred to as *time sharing*. Ownership of a living unit is divided into time intervals, as distinguished from the condominium concept in which the common elements are owned jointly by several owners. Time sharing is designed to provide owners with accommodations for future vacations at today's prices, since it freezes the cost of lodgings at a one time fee stated in the purchase agreement. Because the expense of owning and operating the vacation home is divided among its many users, the cost to each user is less than what it would ordinarily cost to own a vacation home. Time sharing evolved from the rental pool program in which resort apartment owners rented out their apartments when the apartments were not in use to defray and recoup maintenance costs.

In Hawaii, the time-sharing plan can be established in an existing hotel, apartment, or condominium building or in a new resort complex to be constructed. The total number of dwelling units in the building is multiplied by fifty-two weeks to arrive at the total unit weeks that can be sold under the plan.

EXAMPLE: If the developer of the Happy Waikiki Time Share Plan has fifty units in the Happy Waikiki resort complex, the fifty units are multiplied by fifty-two weeks and the developer would thus have 2600 unit weeks available in the complex for sale.

Under the ideal time-sharing plan, the developer achieves what all hotels strive to accomplish—one hundred percent occupancy of all units all year, year after year, during the term of the contract. To attract buyers, the developer packages a long-term agreement for each owner to occupy one of the units for a week or two and guarantees the owner a set rate that cannot be changed during the term of the agreement.

In Hawaii, the statute expressly provides that a time-share interest constitutes "real estate," and the offer and sale of such interest constitutes the offer or sale of an interest in real estate. A sales agent or acquisition agent (a person who, for compensation, solicits or encourages others to attend a time-share sales presentation or to contact a sales agent or developer) is not allowed to sell time share or act as a real estate broker in the sale of time share without previously obtaining a license from the real estate commission.

Each county is authorized to limit the location of time-share units, time-share plans (any plan or program in which the use, occupancy, or possession of one or more time-share units circulates among various occupants, each of whom takes possession for less than a sixty-day period in any one year), and other transient vacation rentals to areas deemed appropriate. Such areas are usually those designated for hotel or resort use or transient vacation rentals.

A developer is prohibited from offering or disposing of a time-share unit or time-share interest without first filing a disclosure statement with the director of the Department of Commerce and Consumer Affairs of the State of Hawaii.

REFERENCE: Time Sharing. Chapter 514E, *Hawaii Revised Statutes*.

A Brief Note on Commercial and Institutional Properties

Commercial properties, commonly referred to as income-producing properties, include apartment and office buildings, retail stores, and warehouses. In acquiring commercial properties, a buyer is usually concerned with income, value appreciation, financing of the purchase, and, until the recently enacted Tax Reform Act, the tax shelter that could reasonably have been expected from ownership of such property. Because commercial properties are generally purchased for investment reasons, knowledge of tax laws and accounting principles is important in order to determine the economic feasibility of acquiring a particular commercial property.

Institutional properties are properties that are used for such purposes as universities, colleges, schools, churches, and hospitals. Such properties are in limited supply. However, in the case of the University of Hawaii, the State of Hawaii may exercise its power of eminent domain to acquire land for university use by condemnation. (We shall discuss eminent domain and condemnation in chapter 23.) Churches and hospitals are restricted to land that is zoned institutional.

IMPORTANT POINT: The rights and responsibilities of the residential real estate owner depend on the type of the property. Be sure you understand what those rights and responsibilities are when you consider purchasing a home.

4 Why Retain a Real Estate Broker?

There is no law that prohibits an unlicensed individual from selling or purchasing his or her own home, or any real estate, for that matter. If such is the case, do you really need to retain a real estate broker? The answer depends on how serious you are about selling or purchasing a home, how attentive you are to all the requirements of a real estate transaction, how quickly you wish to sell or purchase the home, and whether you are able or competent to handle any problem that might arise in the sale or purchase of real estate. Real estate transactions are complex and wrought with pitfalls for the unknowing. Many decisions must be made even before you actually sell or purchase your home, and many things must be done to bring the transaction to a successful consummation.

In order to appreciate the value of retaining a broker, you must first understand the services customarily performed by a real estate broker. Although there are differences between brokers and salespersons, the discussion in this chapter applies to a salesperson as well as a broker. Any distinction that is critical will be pointed out. There is often confusion between the terms "broker" and "realtor," and they are sometimes used interchangeably. In fact, they have separate and distinct meanings. "Broker" is the general term used to describe the person who sells or offers to sell, buys or offers to buy, negotiates the purchase, sale, or exchange, or leases or offers to lease real estate. "Realtor" is a copyrighted and registered term of the National Association of Realtors (NAR), which is the best known of the professional real estate organizations. The word "realtor" is reserved exclusively for members for the NAR. The term applies to a broker, and "realtor-associate" applies to a salesperson working for a member realtor.

What Does a Broker Do?

Simply put, the function of the broker, when representing a seller, is to find a buyer for the property owned by the seller, and, when representing a buyer, it is to find a suitable property meeting the buyer's criteria. However, in today's sophisticated economic world, the broker's job is not that simple. The broker must be knowledgeable about zoning, building codes, taxes, financing, law, advertising, and marketing, as well as general information on real estate and the community in which a property is located.

Many brokers, like doctors and lawyers, are now specialists rather than dealing with all types of real estate. Some specialize in residential properties, others only in commercial and industrial properties, and still others in a specific area, such as Hawaii Kai, the North Shore on Oahu, Kihei, or Kona. These brokers become well versed in their specialties, and they seek out pertinent information in order to be current on facts and statistics relating to the properties in which they specialize. If a broker neglects to tell you his or her specialty, you should ask to be sure that he or she is familiar with the type of property you intend to sell or acquire.

When representing a seller, the broker discusses with the property owner the asking price for his or her property. That price will be based on *comparables,* which are recent sale prices for similar properties in the area. In some instances, an appraiser may be hired to appraise the property to determine its fair market value. (There will be more discussion on appraisers in chapter 6.) Amenities and unique features of the property, such as swimming pools, saunas, lanais, and panoramic views, will be considered in deciding what the asking price ought to be.

The broker may recommend to an owner repairs, refurbishing, or renovations that might be made in order to command a higher price for his property. She will advertise the property in the newspapers and real estate periodicals, and, if she is a member of the Board of Realtors, she will have the property listed in the Multiple Listing Service weekly periodical. She will show the property, on predetermined dates and times or by private arrangement. If the buyer is not represented by his own broker, she prepares the contract to purchase the property. Thereafter, she coordinates with the escrow so that all of the conditions in the contract that must be met are fulfilled by the time the transaction closes. This summary by no means illustrates all the functions that a broker carries out for the seller.

When acting as broker for a buyer, the broker's responsibilities are no fewer than those involved in representing a seller. She must first find out what type of residence the buyer is looking for. She needs to know whether he is interested in a single-family dwelling, a condominium, or a townhouse and, for example, whether he desires a two- or three-bedroom home. The price range he can afford is also critical, because it may determine the areas of the community that are available to the buyer. After learning the criteria of the property sought by the buyer, the broker will review all available information to find properties that suit the buyer's wishes and needs or, if none is available, properties that come close to the buyer's criteria. The buyer together with his broker inspects those properties that are available. The broker's opinions, based on her knowledge and experience, will be helpful to the buyer in determining the positive and negative points of the property.

It is important to note that if a buyer inspects or visits a property without his own broker and fails to inform the seller's broker that he is represented by a broker, the seller's broker may claim the buyer to be her client. When such claim is made, the request by the buyer's broker for payment of her commission may be refused by the seller's broker. Therefore, if you are represented by a broker, you should inform the seller's broker that you are represented by a broker and give the broker's name, if and when you inspect a property on your own.

If a property is found and the buyer is interested in purchasing it, the broker will prepare a contract to purchase the property, and, in so doing, she will discuss with the buyer all the terms and conditions that may need to be included in the contract. In this respect, the broker's experience and knowledge will again be extremely helpful. The purchase price to be tendered to the seller will have the broker's input. Generally, there will be some negotiation on the price. In most cases, the buyer will not agree to pay the full asking price. The broker will recommend a purchase price based on her available information including comparables. It will also take into account any negative features of the property that would cause the price to be less than that of similar properties. If the buyer needs to obtain a loan to pay for the property, the broker will draft the contract so that the buyer will have sufficient time to apply for a loan, have the loan approved by a financial institution, have all legal documents prepared for signing, and fund the loan amount by the time of closing. Unless the buyer is aware of the time required to complete all these matters, the contract may not be drafted properly to give enough time to complete everything, and the transaction may be scheduled to close even before the legal documents can be prepared. If a loan is necessary to purchase the property, the broker may help the buyer obtain a loan at a financial institution whose interest rate is affordable and whose loan terms are advantageous to the buyer. The broker will usually inspect the property on the closing date to be sure that no damage has occurred to the premises since the signing of the contract and that it is in the condition in which the seller agreed to sell it to the buyer. Like the seller's broker, the buyer's broker will also coordinate with the escrow so that all of the contract terms are met before closing. Again, these are but examples of the functions carried out by the buyer's broker and are not exclusive.

How Do You Find a Broker?

As if you were looking for the right doctor for your ailment or the right lawyer for your legal problem, you might start by asking friends and relatives for references. They might suggest brokers, and if those brokers are unable to assist you, they in turn might suggest other brokers who might be able to do so. You might also check the *Yellow Pages* for names of brokers, but before retaining such a broker, or any broker, you should discuss the services you can expect to receive from her, her expertise, her commission, and her familiarity with the kind of property that you are interested in acquiring. Many brokers advertise the properties listed with them in the real estate section of the Sunday edition of the local newspaper. The ads might give you an idea of the types of properties listed with particular brokers and the asking prices for the properties. In fact, you could contact the broker directly if any listed property interested you. However, you must bear in mind that in such a case, there is some question as to whom the broker really represents, because the seller who lists the property for sale with the broker is also represented by the same broker.

Most brokers belong to a professional organization that establishes a standard of professional conduct and ethics. Membership in such an organization is certainly not a guarantee of a broker's professional conduct, but you should inquire whether a broker you are considering retaining is a member of such organization and confirm his membership with the local office of the organization. Any past unprofessional or unethical conduct may have been grounds to cancel his membership.

Is the Broker an Agent?

When you retain a broker, she has certain legal powers. It is important that you know what these powers are so that you will understand the extent to which you are bound by your broker's actions. She is an agent employed to negotiate the sale, purchase, lease, or exchange of real property for compensation, usually a commission, if the transaction is successfully completed. The *principal* is the person who authorizes another individual to act as his representative, and the *agent* is the person who is authorized to act for the principal. The seller is the principal when he hires the broker to sell his property. The buyer is the broker's principal when he employs a broker to represent him in the purchase of real estate.

A broker is considered a *fiduciary* to her principal. A fiduciary is required to be trustworthy and honest and exercise good judgment when performing duties on behalf of her principal. The broker is required to perform her duties and responsibilities faithfully, to be loyal to her principal, and to account for all funds handled by her as a broker. She must keep the principal fully informed with regard to all matters affecting the sale or purchase of a property in question and to promote and protect the principal's interest.

> EXAMPLE: A broker cannot remain silent if she has knowledge that the property listed for sale by her principal, the seller, has a higher value than desired by her principal, and the broker cannot purchase the property under the name of a third party without fully disclosing to the principal what she intends to do. Such a purchase would be a clear breach of fiduciary duty and a conflict of interest.

Is a Broker Licensed?

In Hawaii, as in other states, the statute requires that all real estate brokers and real estate salespersons be licensed by the state. This requirement exists for the protection of the public.

In this state, a broker can be an individual, a partnership, or a corporation owned and operated by an individual who is a licensed broker. The broker may hire other licensed brokers or licensed salespersons to work for him or her.

A real estate salesperson is a person employed directly or indirectly by a broker or an independent contractor in association with a broker to list and negotiate the sale, exchange, lease, or rental of real estate for others under the direction of the broker. Only an individual may be licensed as a salesperson. Moreover, a salesperson must be employed by a broker; he or she cannot operate independently.

The State of Hawaii has established the Real Estate Commission to regulate the real estate licensing procedure, real estate practices, and real estate brokers and salespersons. It has the power to grant licenses and to suspend or revoke any license granted by the commission. Day-to-day activities are administered by the executive secretary of the Real Estate Commission. If after you have retained a broker, you find that she has made a misrepresentation, a false promise, or conducted herself in a manner that you consider fraudulent or dishonest, you may lodge a complaint against the broker with the Real Estate Commission, and it will take the proper course of action against her.

REFERENCE: Real Estate Brokers and Salesmen. Chapter 467, *Hawaii Revised Statutes*.

What Happens in Case of Wrongdoing by a Broker?

In case of a broker's or a salesperson's wrongdoing, the Real Estate Commission has the power to revoke her commission. However, because the revocation of the license will not provide financial compensation for the damages sustained by the wronged party, the Real Estate Commission has established and maintains a real estate recovery fund. Any person aggrieved through an act, representation, transaction, or conduct by a licensed real estate broker or real estate salesperson of fraud, misrepresentation, or deceit may recover from the fund by order of the court not more than $25,000 per transaction for damages sustained, including court costs and fees set by law and reasonable attorney fees. In order to collect from the real estate recovery fund, the legal action on the claim must start no later than two years "from the accrual of the cause of action."

In order to recover from the fund, certain procedural steps must be taken. First, when the aggrieved person commences legal action for a judgment that might result in collection from the recovery fund, the aggrieved person must notify the Real Estate Commission in writing at that time. Then, as a second step, if the aggrieved person obtains a judgment against the real estate broker or salesperson, he may, upon the termination of all judicial proceedings, including reviews and appeals, file a claim in the court in which the judgment was entered. As a third step, after giving ten days written notice to the commission, the aggrieved person may apply to the court for an order directing payment from the recovery fund of the amount unpaid upon the judgment. The liability of the recovery fund for any one licensee is limited to $50,000. As noted earlier, the most that an aggrieved person can recover against a broker is $25,000. If there already have been payments in excess of $50,000 against the same broker, the recovery fund will not pay the aggrieved person.

IMPORTANT POINT: You could, if you wish, sell or purchase real estate on your own. However, it might take you longer to accomplish your goal, because you might have to learn as you proceed. It might prove to be a trial-and-error process, and too many errors could result in a law suit brought against you. It may be more prudent to retain a real estate broker, who can assist you and relieve you of the many responsibilities involved in the sale or purchase of a home. The broker's knowledge and experience can smooth the way to a successful closing of the sale. Statistics indicate that, in more cases than not, real estate brokers or salespersons are involved in Hawaii real estate transactions.

5 Should You List Your Property for Sale?

Now and then, owners attempt to sell their property without the services of a real estate broker, mainly in order to save on the brokerage commission. Because the commission is generally paid from the proceeds realized from the sale of the property, the amount of the commission will be subtracted from the sale proceeds. In order to avoid payment of the brokerage commission, an owner may decide to sell his property on his own. However, the sale of real estate is a complicated and sophisticated matter involving many details, and unless you are experienced and knowledgeable in this area, you may find yourself spending more time and money than if you had retained the services of a professional to assist you.

Once you have decided to seek the services of a real estate broker, the next question is whether to list your property with that broker. A *real estate listing* is an employment contract between a property owner and a real estate broker in which the owner appoints the broker as his or her agent to find a buyer (or a lessee or tenant if the contract involves a lease) for the property on the terms and conditions desired by the owner. Without a listing, the owner is not obligated to deal with one broker. The broker, however, will have more incentive to commit his or her time, money, and effort in the sale of the property if there is a listing agreement with the owner. The essential elements of a listing agreement are as follows:

1. The description and address of the property to be sold.

EXAMPLE: Two bedrooms, fee-simple condominium at the Nani Kai, 8765 Ala Wai Boulevard, Honolulu, Hawaii.

2. The price, terms, and conditions under which the broker is instructed to find a buyer.

EXAMPLE: Listing price $200,000, cash sale, sale must close within sixty days after offer is accepted.

3. The period of time during which the listing is to be in effect. In Hawaii, the customary listing term for residences is ninety days to six months.
4. The amount of the commission to be paid to the broker. The commission is generally a set percentage of the sales price. In Hawaii, the commission for residential properties has traditionally been 6 percent of the sales price. However, there is no legal prohibition of agreement by the owner and broker on a higher or lower percentage or other ways of paying the commission.

EXAMPLE: Rather than a percentage commission, the parties could agree on a dollar amount: 6 percent of $180,000 is $10,800. The owner and broker could decide on a commission of $10,000 rather than $10,800.

A broker earns her commission only when she has completed the job she was hired to perform. If a broker submits an offer signed by a buyer for the full purchase price listed by the seller, the seller under normal conditions would have no reason to refuse the offer. Legally, the seller need not accept the offer inasmuch as the offer is merely an offer to buy. However, since the broker has performed what she was hired to do and has produced a "ready, willing, and able" buyer, the broker has earned her commission and is entitled under the listing agreement to be paid that commission by the seller even if the seller changes his mind and refuses to accept the buyer's offer. Moreover, there is also a law to support a broker's demand for payment of commission from the seller in situations where both the seller and buyer sign a contract, and later the buyer refuses to complete the transaction.

5. The broker's promise to make a reasonable effort to find a buyer.

6. Usually, a provision that if the broker is still working with a prospective buyer at the end of the listing period, the broker is given a specific time period to conclude the sale. In most instances, at the end of the listing period, the broker must disclose to the seller the prospective buyer's name for the broker to receive credit for bringing the buyer to the seller.

7. Authorization to work with other brokers. The seller authorizes the broker to work with other brokers to market the property. The other brokers will be subagents of the seller, and the broker will share her commission with the subagents. In the case in which the other broker represents the buyer, that broker is the buyer's agent, and the seller's broker will share her commission with the buyer's agent.

8. The date of the agreement.

9. The signatures of the seller and the broker.

The major types of listing agreements include the exclusive-right-to-sell listing, the exclusive agency listing, the open listing, and the net listing.

Exclusive-right-to-sell-listing. Under the most widely used practice, the listing broker is entitled to a commission no matter who sells the property during the listing period. The advantage to the seller is that the broker is more willing to spend money and effort advertising and showing the property under this type of arrangement than in other types of listing agreements. The broker earns a commission regardless who brings in the buyer.

Exclusive agency listing. The difference between this type of listing and the exclusive-right-to-sell listing is that the owner may sell the property himself during the listing period and need not pay the brokerage commission to the broker if he sells the property himself. However, the appointed broker is the only broker who can act as the owner's agent during the listing period.

Open listing. Under this arrangement, the owner gives a listing to any number of brokers at the same time, and the owner may find a buyer for his property himself and thus avoid paying a commission to any of the listing brokers if he is able to do so. None of the brokers has an exclusive right to sell.

> EXAMPLE: The owner of a property on Kalakaua Avenue in Waikiki that is highly sought after by many interested investors may not wish to enter into an exclusive-right-to-sell listing or even an exclusive agency listing, because the owner may wish to have as many brokers as possible seeking buyers for the property. In such a case, the owner will have an open listing for his property.

Net listing. In a net listing, the owner states the sale price that he wants for his property and agrees that anything over the sale price is to be paid to the broker as her commission. A net listing can take the form of an exclusive-right-to-sell listing, exclusive agency listing, or open listing.

> EXAMPLE: If an owner asks for a ''net $200,000'' as his sale price and the broker were to sell the property for $215,000, the broker's commission would be $15,000.

Once you decide to list your property for sale with a broker, you should discuss the type of listing agreement that he or she wishes to enter into with you in order to avoid a misunderstanding in the future. Most brokers are happy to discuss the alternatives that are available. The more listings that a broker has means the more inventory she has to sell. Consequently, the listing of properties is a vital part of the real estate brokerage business.

> IMPORTANT POINT: In Hawaii, in the sale of residences, the listing agreement is pretty much standardized, and the agreement is prepared and printed by the Board of Realtors.

6 Should You Hire an Appraiser?

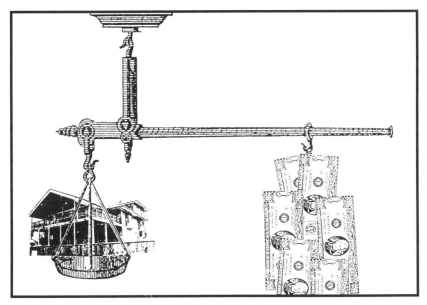

In the previous chapters, we have seen that in most real estate transactions the seller and the buyer of property retain their own real estate brokers to assist them in the sale and purchase of the property. Do you, as seller or buyer, need any other professional assistance? As a rule of thumb, the more complicated the transaction or the higher the price of the property to be purchased or sold, the more important it is to retain other professionals to protect your interests.

When a real estate owner decides to sell his property, one of the most important pieces of information that he needs to know is the fair market value of the property in order to determine a selling price. In the case of a buyer, he or she would wish to know the fair market value in order not to overpay for the property. Learning how much a property is worth is an important part of the decision-making process in selling or buying real estate. The seller, the buyer, or both of them together may wish to seek the services of a real estate appraiser who would appraise the property in question. To *appraise* simply means to estimate the value.

The discussion in this chapter is to familiarize you with appraisers and the work they perform. As a word of caution, in the purchase or sale of the average home, an appraiser is generally not hired by the purchaser or the seller. However, if the purchase is to be financed by a loan, the bank or savings and loan company hires an appraiser to determine the fair market value of the home for loan purposes. In other words, the appraisal is made to determine whether there is sufficient value in the property to support the loan.

Fair market value is defined as the highest monetary price that a property will bring if (1) payment is made in cash or its equivalent, (2) the property is exposed on the open market for a reasonable length of time, (3) the seller and the buyer are fully informed of market conditions and the uses to which the property may be put, (4) neither is under abnormal pressure to conclude the transaction, and (5) the seller is capable of conveying marketable title to the property. Generally, there are three methods for appraising real property: the market approach, the cost approach, and the income approach.

Market Approach. The market approach is to compare similar properties that have sold recently and to use their sales prices, referred to as comparables, as a guide in estimating the value of the property that is being appraised.

> EXAMPLE: If the property (a single-family residence) being appraised is a one-story, redwood frame house in Pearl City consisting of 1,500 square feet and containing three bedrooms, two bathrooms, a living room, a kitchen and dining room, and a two-car carport, the appraiser would seek single-family residences with similar physical features and amenities that were sold recently in Pearl City or its vicinity and use their sale prices as a guide in estimating the fair market value of the property being appraised.

The appraiser seeks information from recorded deeds, assignments of lease, and agreements of sale at the Bureau of Conveyances. Such information includes the dates of the transactions, the locations of the real property, the financing terms, and the sale prices. Whereas an agreement-of-sale document will ordinarily state the sale price, the deed and assignment of lease will not. However, since the law requires a conveyance tax to be paid whenever real property is sold or leased on a long-term basis, the amount of the conveyance tax is a clue to the sale price. Currently, the rate of the conveyance tax is five cents on each $100 of actual and full consideration. Thus, if the price is $100,000, the conveyance tax is $50 ($100,000 divided by $100 is $1,000; $1,000 multiplied by $0.05 is $50). Conversely, if the conveyance tax stamps on the document show that $50 was paid, the sale price can be determined ($50 divided by $0.05 is $1,000; $1,000 multiplied by $100 is $100,000). Records of past sales can also be obtained from real estate title companies and from the Real Property Section of the county tax offices. In Hawaii, Multiple Listing Services also maintains the current records of sales for its subscribers.

The appraiser will base his estimate on three to five comparables, adjusting each comparable for the differences in physical features, amenities, and time sold in relation to the residence being appraised because no two properties are identical.

Cost Approach. The cost approach is to add all the costs of the individual components of the property being appraised. The appraiser includes the cost of a parcel of vacant land similar to the one being appraised, the cost of the structural materials of the home on the property, and construction costs of a similar building. The depreciation of the building is then subtracted from the total cost of the land and building to arrive at the valuation.

EXAMPLE: To find the fair market value of a residential property in Wailuku, Maui, the following steps would be used:

Estimate the value of the land, as though vacant		$100,000
Estimate the present cost of constructing a similar building	$100,000	
Subtract the depreciation	(20,000)	
Add the value of the building		$80,000
Appraised property value based on cost approach		$180,000

In estimating the construction costs, the appraiser must decide whether the estimate will be based on a reproduction basis or on a replacement basis. *Reproduction cost* refers to the cost of constructing an exact replica of the building to be appraised using the same or similar materials. In our example, the appraiser would compute construction costs using the current prices of materials needed to construct the residential structure in Wailuku. *Replacement cost* is the cost of a structure having the same or equivalent usefulness of the property being appraised using current methods of construction at present prices. The replacement cost method is more practical, because it takes into consideration current construction materials and methods and eliminates obsolete features. It may also result in considerable savings due to newer technologies in construction.

Another method for estimating construction costs is the cost-per-square-foot approach. Under this fast and simple approach, the appraiser finds a newly constructed structure of similar size, design, materials, and quality to the structure on the property being appraised and uses this structure as the basis for determining the cost of constructing a new structure. The cost of the recently constructed structure is converted to a cost per square foot by dividing the construction cost by the number of square feet in the structure.

EXAMPLE:

Total construction cost	$200,000
Total square feet in the structure	2,000
$200,000 divided by 2,000 sq. ft.	$100/sq. ft.

The basis for a standard structure would be $100 per square foot. If the property to be appraised consisted of 1,500 square feet, the appraiser would multiply 1,500 square feet by $100 to arrive at $150,000 as the estimated construction cost of the structure being appraised.

Income Approach. The income approach considers the amount of net income that a property can reasonably be expected to produce as well as any anticipated increase or decrease in price. In other words, this approach considers the expected monetary return from a property in light of the return on an investment currently being demanded by investors. The formula is *value equals income divided by rate of return*.

EXAMPLE: Suppose a commercial property in Kapaa, Kauai, produces a net rental income of $12,000 per year to an investor, and any time the investor wants to withdraw his original investment, it will be returned to him in full. The value of his investment depends on the rate of return that must be paid to attract new investors. If an investor is willing to accept a 10 percent per year return on his investment, he would pay $120,000 for this investment opportunity.

Income divided by rate of return equals value
$12,000 ÷ .10 = $120,000

The process of calculating the value of an investment is referred to as *capitalizing the income stream*. *Capitalize* means to convert future income to current value. In our illustration, the capitalized value of the $12,000 net annual income is $120,000.

In the income approach, it is critical to project the net income as accurately as possible, because even a one dollar error will make a difference in the market value of the property. Appraisers computing net income will generally review actual records of the income and expenses of the property being appraised over a period of three to five years. In most instances, the past record (historical record) is the best guide to future performance of the property.

Which of the three approaches to choose depends to a great extent on the type of real property being appraised. Because most homes are not purchased for income generating purposes, the appraiser will generally use the market and cost approaches. If all three approaches are used, the appraiser will reconcile the market, cost, and income approaches by assigning to each approach a weighting factor based on the appraiser's judgment of which of the approaches are the most relevant in valuing the property.

You must bear in mind that this is a simplified explanation of the appraiser's work. In actuality, it is a more complicated procedure. Furthermore, real estate appraisal is not an exact science. It is a professional's best estimate of the value of a specific real estate at a given date. It is subjective, and therefore, it is not surprising to find different valuations placed by different appraisers on the same real property.

At this point, we should also touch upon the factors that create value in a property. Generally, value is created by demand, utility, scarcity, and transferability.

> EXAMPLE: If we were to value an ocean front lot in Kailua-Kona, demand would mean the need or desire for such property together with the financial ability to fulfill it. Utility would be the ability of the lot to fill the need. Scarcity would refer to the short supply of ocean front lots in Kailua-Kona and transferability to the ability to convey the property with relative ease from the owner to another person.

An appraiser may be requested to appraise a property for a reason other than to determine the fair market value. He may be asked to render his opinion on a value based on the *highest and best use* of a property, that is, its greatest current value. For instance, if the property to be appraised is a fifty-year-old single-family dwelling in Waikiki, the fair market value of the land and the dwelling is considerably less than the property at its highest and best use. The use to which that property is presently put is not the use that makes the land the most valuable, since most of the surrounding lands are improved with hotels, condominiums and commercial buildings. Therefore, the value of the property at its highest and best use would be the value of the land as improved with a hotel, condominium, or commercial building.

There are two well-known professional appraisal organizations. One is the American Institute of Real Estate Appraisers (AIREA), and the other is the Society of Real Estate Appraisers. Both organizations have developed a designation system to recognize appraisal education, experience, and competence. The highest designation within the AIREA is the MAI (Member of the Appraisal Institute). The SREA (Senior Real Estate Analyst) and SRPA (Senior Real Property Appraiser) are the most advanced designations in the Society of Real Estate Appraisers.

IMPORTANT POINT: In the average sale or purchase of residential real estate, it is not necessary to hire an appraiser to determine the fair market value of the property. Your real estate broker should have enough information, based on past sales, to advise you whether a price is fair or not.

7 What Other Professional Assistance Do You Need?

There are other professionals besides the real estate broker and appraiser whom you may wish to consult in a real estate transaction. They include a certified public accountant, an architect or engineer, a surveyor, and an attorney.

Certified Public Account

When purchasing or selling real estate, it may be prudent to consult with a certified public account (C.P.A.) or a tax attorney regarding the impact of tax laws on the transaction. The Tax Reform Act of 1986 (TRA) made sweeping changes in the federal income tax laws that you will need to understand. If you are selling a residence, for instance, it is important to decide when to purchase another residence. If the other residence is bought within a designated period, under the federal tax laws, you will not be obligated to pay any capital gains tax on the capital gains you may have earned in the sale of your home. The sale of your home and the purchase of a new home require coordination and timing on your part.

When buying or selling real estate, consult a C.P.A. even at the exploratory stage, because tax considerations may be a critical factor regarding when the property should be purchased or sold and the terms and conditions that ought to be negotiated as part of the contract. Note that the Tax Reform Act ends the preferential treatment of a long-term capital gain. Under the new law, capital gains are taxed at the same rate as ordinary income.

Prior to the Tax Reform Act, tax planning was an important consideration for the buyer purchasing real estate for investment purposes, because the purchase may have served as a *tax shelter.* A tax shelter is an income tax savings that an investor can realize, because part of the income from the investment is not subject to taxation. The Tax Reform Act has taken away the numerous advantages of tax shelters. Under TRA, there has been a crackdown on tax shelter losses. Generally, a taxpayer is allowed to write off a tax shelter loss only against other tax shelter income. The new tax law prevents a taxpayer from using a loss from a "passive activity" (a business or investment in which the taxpayer is not involved on a regular, continuous, and substantial basis) to shelter "active income" (for example, salary) or "portfolio income" (dividends, interest, and capital gains). However, there is an exception to this rule. The law allows the first $25,000 of loss for rental real estate to offset income from any source.

The new law reduces the credit for rehabilitating certain types of buildings. As a general rule, there are only two credits remaining after 1986. Neither is applicable to most homeowners. One is a 20 percent credit for historic structures. The other is a 10 percent credit for industrial and commercial properties built before 1936.

Although many of the former tax savings features are no longer available, a few of the former tax credits were retained in the Tax Reform Act. For instance, depreciation of an investment property is still deductible. The rate of depreciation is now 27.5 years for residential rental property and 31.5 years for commercial property.

In short, a C.P.A. should be consulted on the benefits and disadvantages, timing, and strategy of an investment to be made. Some of the benefits of real estate investment include cash flow, tax shelter, leverage (ability to acquire property with only a down payment), and property appreciation. The expertise of a C.P.A. is helpful in computing and analyzing how these benefits can best be realized.

Architect or Engineer

Ordinarily, if you are acquiring a single-family dwelling or even a condominium apartment in a highrise structure, it is not necessary for you, as the buyer, to retain the service of an architect or an engineer to check on the structural condition of the residence or building. In most instances, except for normal wear and tear of the structure and the settling of the residence or building, there should be no structural problem that would cause a major problem for the purchaser. However, you may wish to determine the condition of the soil on which the structure is constructed. If the soil is adobe or the ground of surrounding properties has shifted, you should hire an architect or engineer to check the structure for any defects that are apparent or may become a problem.

There are certain areas along hillsides on Oahu, such as Manoa, Palolo, Aina Haina, and Kuliouou, where ground shifting has caused damage to existing homes. In these and any other areas, if in doubt, consult an engineer and get his opinion of the soil conditions. An inquiry now can prevent a lot of grief later on.

Surveyor

It is important that the boundary measurements of your land be as accurate as possible, particularly in urban areas where every square inch of land is extremely valuable. You want to be sure that your property includes all the land to which you are entitled.

In most real estate contracts in Hawaii, the buyer requests and the seller agrees to pay for the cost of staking by a licensed surveyor if stakes (boundary pins) are not already visible. If the buyer orders a survey to be conducted, the seller reimburses the buyer for the cost of the survey only if the original stakes prove to be inaccurate. An accurate boundary survey is important when purchasing real property, because the purchaser does not wish to buy a lawsuit. She could be faced with one later if she were to purchase a property with a boundary line dispute.

Attorney

It is not the usual practice in Hawaii to hire an attorney to review the contract or the legal documents involved in the purchase of residential real estate. Some mainland states require that an attorney review the legal documents at the closing of a residential real estate transaction, but there is no similar requirement in Hawaii.

Although the majority of real estate transactions in Hawaii are negotiated and closed without the services of an attorney, not all transactions are without any legal problems. Situations in which you ought to consult with an attorney are (1) investment in a general partnership that will own real estate, because all of your assets as a general partner will be exposed to execution (seizure) or attachment in case of a judgment against the partnership; (2) conversion of an existing building into a condominium; (3) bidding at public auctions of foreclosed properties; (4) purchasing real property from the developer of a project who may be in financial difficulties, as there may be liens and judgments on the property; and (5) in other situations where there may be a "cloud" over the real estate to be purchased. When in doubt, consult with an attorney *before* signing the contract. After it is signed, a buyer is not able to cancel the contract in most cases, unless fraud or other inequitable causes have been perpetrated by the seller or his broker. In a litigious society such as ours, it is difficult to back out of a contract without considerable effort and the payment of some money.

> IMPORTANT POINT: Besides consulting professionals before signing a contract to purchase a home, it is always worth your while to talk to the neighbors on adjoining properties and inquire whether there is anything about the property that you ought to know. You may be surprised to learn things about the property that may not be obvious to you or your broker.

8 Who Are the Seller and the Buyer?

All real estate transactions involve a seller and a buyer. In order for the transaction to be consummated successfully, it must be valid and binding on both parties to the transaction, the seller and the buyer. As a party to a transaction, you ought to know who the other party is, because certain legal requirements may arise depending on the parties to the transaction.

Legal Competence

Under contract law, a party to a contract must have the capacity to enter into a contract. Unless a person is legally competent to make a contract, the contract will not be enforceable against that person. In other words, if a party to a contract does not have the capacity to understand or agree to the terms and conditions of the contract, the courts will not require that person to live up to the contract.

Legal incapacity may be attributable to nonage, as in the case of infants or minors, or mental aberration, permanent or temporary, as in cases of insanity or drunkenness. The law deems a minor to lack the legal capacity to enter into a contract. In Hawaii, the age of majority, that is, the age when a minor becomes an adult, is eighteen years. In most states, a contract made by a minor is voidable (cancellable) at the option of the minor. In other states, the contract is simply void, that is, the contract has no legal force or binding effect. Hawaii follows the minority view that a contract made by a minor is void.[1]

Even if a contract is voidable at the option of the minor, he or she may enforce the contract against an adult. Also, there is nothing to prohibit the minor from ratifying (affirming) the contract after reaching the age of majority. Although a minor has the right to disaffirm the contract, he or she is liable for the return or the value of any tangible benefits received under the contract and still in his or her possession. Because in most jurisdictions a minor may disaffirm a contract even if she has misrepresented her age, it is advisable when dealing with a young person to verify his or her age.

A word of caution to anyone considering a transfer of real estate as a gift to a minor: Although there is nothing wrong with making a gift to a minor, there may be some inconvenience later if the real estate is sold by the minor, because he will lack the legal capacity to enter into a contract. In such cases, it will be necessary for the court to appoint a guardian to sign the contract on behalf of the minor. The court appointment will require time and effort and will cost money.

EXAMPLE: Grandfather Moke conveys a parcel of land to his favorite granddaughter, Alice, who is fifteen years old. When Alice becomes seventeen years old and is ready to enter college, her father does not have enough money to pay for her college expenses, and, consequently, the gift from Alice's grandfather must be sold. However, because she is still a minor, an adult (most likely her father or mother) must be appointed as her guardian to sign the contract to sell the land.

Mental incompetence is another instance in which a contract may be voided based on lack of legal capacity. A person is held to be incompetent when the person does not understand the nature, purpose, and consequences of his act at the time of the transaction. Thus, a person suffering from mental illness and defect would be mentally incompetent to enter into a contract. The individual need not be suffering from permanent mental illness but only be mentally ill at the time he enters into the contract. A contract made by a person who is lacking in mental capacity is voidable by that person or his representative.

A contract is voidable if one party is unable to act in a reasonable way in connection with the transaction, and the other person knows of this condition. Intoxicated and drugged persons fall under this category. It is immaterial that the drunkenness may have been voluntary and was not procured by means of the other party to the contract. The contract, although voidable at the option of the intoxicated person, is binding on the other party.

> EXAMPLE: Egbert Wobblylegs patronizes the Happiness Forever Cocktail Lounge and consumes a liter of wine. He becomes intoxicated. Any written promise by him to sell his real estate during his intoxication is not enforceable against him, because the law will deem that he lacked the mental capacity to enter into a contract.

Individual

When the seller or buyer with whom you are dealing is an individual, the individual's signature is all that is required to have a binding contract. However, in instances when the seller or buyer are multiple parties, all of the parties need to sign the contract to have a valid, enforceable contract. Otherwise, the contract is not enforceable against the person who has not signed the contract.

> EXAMPLE: Arnold and Betty Rocker are owners of real estate in Kaneohe. Arnold signs a contract to sell the property to Charlie Yama. Arnold tells Charlie, "Don't worry, Betty signs whatever I tell her to sign." Betty refuses to go through with the transaction. Charlie cannot compel Betty to sign the documents to complete the transaction, because Betty did not sign the contract to sell the real estate to Charlie in the first place.

EXAMPLE: A parcel of land is owned by twenty individuals each of whom owns a 1/20 interest in the land. The buyer of the land acquires only the interest of those individuals who sign the contract to sell their interest to the buyer. Those owners who do not sign the contract remain owners of the land, retaining their fractional interest. Therefore, if seventeen people agree to sell their interest, the buyer acquires a 17/20 interest in the land, and the other three owners retain a 3/20 interest in the property.

Corporation

A *corporation* has been defined by the United States Supreme Court as "an artificial being, invisible, intangible, and existing only in contemplation of law." It is an association of persons to whom the state has offered a franchise to become an artificial person with a name of its own under which it can act and contract and sue and be sued. Among the powers, privileges, and immunities granted to the corporation by the state are continuous legal identity and perpetual succession under the corporate name, regardless of successive changes by death of members in the corporation. Therefore, unless the charter of the corporation limits its existence to a definite period of time, the existence of a corporation is perpetual and continues until dissolved by its stockholders.

A corporation is an entity separate and distinct from its individual members, the stockholders, who are natural persons. The ownership of the property and assets of the corporation is vested in the corporation itself and not in the stockholders. The stockholders do not have the power to represent or act for the corporation in their capacity as stockholders nor are the stockholders personally liable for the obligations and debts of the corporation.

EXAMPLE: Tom, Dick, and Harry form a Hawaii corporation, TODIHA Corporation, which purchases a subdivision lot on Molokai. Legally, as stockholders, Tom, Dick, and Harry own shares of stock in TODIHA Corporation. They do not own the Molokai property; the corporation does. The seller of the Molokai property cannot sue Tom, Dick, and Harry if TODIHA Corporation is unable to pay for the subdivision property, because they are not personally liable.

The authority of a corporation to enter into contracts is vested exclusively in its board of directors, which manages the affairs of the corporation. Generally, the board of directors has full and complete discretion in determining whether the corporation should enter into a contract.

Actions of the shareholders and board of directors take the form of corporate resolutions. When a corporation sells or purchases real estate, the other party to the transaction will generally request as part of the conditions of the sale, a "certificate of resolution" authorizing the corporation to enter into the real estate transaction.

REFERENCES: Hawaii Business Corporation Act. Chapter 415, *Hawaii Revised Statutes.* Also, Foreign Corporations. Chapter 418, *Hawaii Revised Statutes.*

Partnership

The Hawaii statute defines a *partnership* as "an association (including a joint venture) of two or more persons to carry on as co-owners a business for profit." A partnership is clearly distinguishable from a corporation. A corporation is an artificial person created by law to be the representative of the persons who become holders of shares in the corporation. The corporation, in turn, owns property and assets. Whereas shareholders are not liable personally for corporate obligations or debts, each partner is individually liable for the obligations and debts of a partnership and for the acts of the other partners, so far as those acts are within the scope of their authority as partners. Moreover, each member, as a principal, can bind the partnership. No shareholder as such can bind a corporation, because an act of the corporation requires the action of the board of directors. Also, one individual shareholder can own a corporation, but a single individual cannot form a partnership. A final distinction is the duration of the partnership. Whereas a corporation's existence may be perpetual, the duration of a partnership is fixed for a certain time, and, upon the expiration of the term, the partnership is dissolved. A partnership also dissolves upon the death of a partner.

There are two types of partnership: the *general partnership* and the *limited partnership.* The limited partnership is defined in the statute as "a partnership formed by two or more persons . . . having as members one or more general partners and one or more limited partners." The definition continues: "The limited partners as such shall not be bound by the obligations of the partnership." In contrast to general partners, who are liable for the debts and obligations of the partnership, a limited partner's liability generally extends to the amount of his or her partnership contribution. A limited partner is sometimes referred to as a silent partner.

EXAMPLE: If Sam Silencio invests $5,000 as his capital contribution to a partnership as a limited partner, his liability will be limited to $5,000.

Persons desiring to form a limited partnership are required to sign and file a certificate stating certain information with the Department of Commerce and Consumer Affairs.

EXAMPLE: Tom, Dick, and Harry tell Sam Silencio, "We will form a limited partnership with you as a limited partner and the rest of us will be general partners. As partners, we will buy a Waikiki condominium." Sam asks, "Do I need to sign any legal papers saying I am only a limited partner?" The others say, "Don't worry about it. We'll take care of everything." No limited partnership certificate is signed. The law deems Sam Silencio to be a general partner, and he is liable as a general partner.

Under the current Hawaii statute, the acquisition and transfer of real property by a partnership has been simplified. Although there may be a number of partners, it is not necessary to acquire the real property in the name of all of the partners. It can be purchased in the name of the partnership and later sold in the partnership name, thus reducing the number of signatures on the conveyance document. Only one authorized partner in a general partnership or one general partner in a limited partnership need sign the conveyance instrument.

EXAMPLE: If real property is sold to a limited partnership with ten partners whose partnership name is Hawaii Ten Partners, the property will be conveyed to Hawaii Ten Partners and the contract to purchase will be signed as follows:

Hawaii Ten Partners, a registered Hawaii limited partnership

By   (Name of Partner)

    Its Authorized General Partner

REFERENCE: Partnerships. Chapter 425, *Hawaii Revised Statutes.*

Trusts

A trust is an arrangement whereby property, real or personal, is transferred from one person (the settlor) to another (the trustee) with the intention that the trustee hold title to the property and be subject to certain duties with respect to the property for the benefit of another (the beneficiary). The trust property is referred to as the *trust res.*

> EXAMPLE: Steve Success has worked all his life and has accumulated vast real estate holdings. He wishes his wife, Sylvia, to be properly taken care of, especially after his death. He is told that a trust company could provide the necessary professional services to manage the holdings. Therefore, Steve transfers some of the real estate to 50th State Trust Company, Inc. for the benefit of Sylvia, with the trustee's services beginning immediately after the transfer. In this case, Steve is the settlor, 50th State Trust Company, Inc., is the trustee, and Sylvia is the beneficiary.

Trusts are classified as *testamentary trusts,* which become effective after the death of the settlor, and *inter vivos trusts* or *living trusts,* which are effective during the life of the settlor. Steve Success in the example has created a living trust.

Most trusts are created intentionally by the settlor by signing a written document, such as a trust instrument, will, or deed. Trusts so created are known as *express trusts.* In certain situations, a trust may arise by operation of law. Such a trust can be either a *resulting trust* or a *constructive trust*. The latter trust comes into existence when the law implies an intention to create a trust, and sometimes irrespective of an intention to create a trust. The constructive trust, for instance, could be a remedy to prevent unjust enrichment by a person possessing a property. In this book, we will focus our attention on express trusts.

Anyone competent to enter into contract may make a disposition of the legal title to his property, with such conditions and limitations as he chooses, to a trustee. A valid trust cannot exist without terms and conditions attached to the transfer of the property; otherwise, the transfer would constitute an absolute disposition of property, such as a sale or gift, and not a trust.

A trust may be created for any legal purpose or to achieve any objective that is not contrary to public policy. Purposes for creating a trust include collection of income and rent, payment of creditors and mortgagees, management of property, operation of a business, protection of beneficiaries against creditors, or conservation of property pending its disposition.

A trust in which real property is the trust asset is governed by the law of the place where the property is located.

> EXAMPLE: A trust is established in Hawaii with a trustee who resides in Hawaii, but the real property is located in California. Any questions relating to the California property must be interpreted under California law.

It is essential in the creation and existence of a trust that there be a competent trustee. However, if the person nominated as trustee is incompetent, disqualified, or refuses to accept the position of trustee, the court will appoint a trustee if an alternative trustee is not named in the trust instrument.

Hawaii has adopted the Uniform Trustees' Powers Act, which confers upon the trustee powers too numerous to list here. The act protects third persons dealing with a trustee, by providing that the existence of trust powers and the proper exercise of those powers by the trustee may be assumed without inquiry. The third person is not bound to inquire whether the trustee has the power to act or is properly exercising that power.

The trustee is deemed by law to be a fiduciary. He or she must observe the standards in dealing with the trust assets that would be observed by a prudent person dealing with the property of another. If the trustee has special skills or is named trustee on the basis of representations of special skills or expertise, she is under a duty to use those skills.

A trustee signs in the trustee's capacity, even if she holds title to the property.

EXAMPLE: Harriet Honesto is the trustee of a trust in which Yvonne Minor Young is the beneficiary. Harriet holds the title to the trust property as a trustee. When the trust property is sold by Harriet, as trustee, Harriet signs as follows:

/s/ Harriet Honesto
_____

Harriet Honesto
Trustee of that certain Yvonne
Minor Young Trust dated
January 1, 1980

REFERENCES: Trust Administration. Uniform Probate Code, Article VII, Chapter 560, *Hawaii Revised Statutes*. Also, Uniform Trustees' Powers Act. Chapter 554A, *Hawaii Revised Statutes*.

Guardian

A *guardianship* is a relationship in which one person, called the *guardian,* acts for another, called the *ward* or *protected person,* who is incapable of managing his property or affairs. A guardian may be appointed to control the property and person of the ward, only the property, or only the person. In Hawaii, the minor or person for whom a guardian of the property has been appointed is referred to as a protected person, and a person for whom a guardian of the person has been appointed is known as a ward. An *incapacitated person* is defined in the statutes to be "any person who is impaired by reason of mental illness, mental deficiency, physical illness or disability, advanced age, chronic use of drugs, chronic intoxication, or other cause (except minority) to the extent that the person lacks sufficient understanding or capacity to make or communicate responsible decisions concerning one's person."[2]

In Hawaii, the Family Court has jurisdiction over guardianships involving the person (the ward or the incapacitated person), and the regular Circuit Court has jurisdiction over the property of the protected person. The parents of a minor are the natural guardians of the minor, and they need not be appointed as guardians. If, however, both parents were to die, a court appointment of a guardian of the person of the minor is required and a guardian of his or her property would be required should the minor own any property.

Once a person is appointed guardian, he or she remains under the jurisdiction of and is accountable to the court. He may be required to file periodic accounting reports to the court. The court appointing the guardian retains jurisdiction for all purposes relating to the guardianship until the guardian is legally discharged.

The selection of the person to be appointed guardian is left to the discretion of the court. The wishes of a parent, often stated in the parent's will, are given primary consideration. A person nominated under the will of a testator (a person making a will) is known as a *testamentary guardian*. The law provides that in the appointment of a guardian of a ward "any competent person whose appointment will be in the best interest of the minor" shall be given the primary consideration of the court. The court may consider the business acumen, morals, character, and conduct of an appointee as well as the probability of his being able to exercise the powers and duties of guardian for the full period of the guardianship.

In those instances where the guardian acts as the guardian of the property of the minor or protected person, he is entitled to the possession and control of the estate of the minor or protected person. Title or ownership, however, continues with the minor or protected person. Such a guardian will be appointed in the following instances: (1) if the court determines that a minor owns money or property that requires management or protection that cannot otherwise be provided, has or may have business affairs that may be jeopardized or prevented by his or her minority, or needs funds for support and education that such protection would provide; or (2) if the court determines that (i) the person is unable to manage his or her property and affairs effectively for reasons of mental illness, mental deficiency, physical illness or disability, advanced age, chronic use of drugs, chronic intoxication, confinement, detention by a foreign power, disappearance, or other incapacity; and (ii) the person has property that will be wasted or dissipate unless proper management is provided or needs funds for the support, care, and welfare of the person or those entitled to be supported by the person that such protection would provide or make possible to obtain.

Title to the property is not transferred to the guardian as it would be to a trustee. The ward or the protected person continues to hold title to the property. However, when real estate is purchased or sold, the guardian signs in the capacity of guardian.

REFERENCES: Protection of Persons Under Disability and Their Property. Article V, Chapter 560, *Hawaii Revised Statutes*. Also, Guardians and Wards. Chapter 551, *Hawaii Revised Statutes*.

Power of Attorney

A *power of attorney* is a written authorization signed by one person, called the principal, appointing another person as her agent to perform certain acts on behalf of the principal. The agent is called the *attorney-in-fact*. The legal instrument called the power of attorney is evidence of the attorney-in-fact's authorization to act on behalf of the principal to a third person. Without such an instrument, a third person has no way of verifying the power of the attorney-in-fact to bind the principal. A power of attorney is often used when the principal may not be present to sign a legal document on a designated date.

> EXAMPLE: Barbara V. Busy will be out of town on July 1, the date set for the real estate closing. She appoints her trusted friend Gloria Goodheart to be her attorney-in-fact to sign all documents required for the closing. She does so through a power of attorney.

There are two types of power of attorney: *general power of attorney* and *special power of attorney*. In a general power of attorney, the attorney-in-fact has the authority to act on all assets owned by the principal, including but not restricted to real estate, cash, stocks, bonds, jewelry, and cars, as though the principal were acting on her own. Put another way, the attorney-in-fact deals with the principal's property as though it were his own. Because the attorney in fact can act freely without restriction, it is extremely important that the person selected to act as attorney-in-fact under a general power of attorney be honest and trustworthy. The special power of attorney restricts the power and authority of the attorney-in-fact to specific assets or to certain functions and responsibilities.

> EXAMPLE: The following is a special power of attorney: "I hereby authorize my attorney-in-fact, Royden Reliable, to negotiate for the purchase of and execute the contract for the purchase of that certain real property located at 9876 Wainiha Street, Honolulu, Hawaii. This authorization shall expire and shall be of no force and effect three (3) months after the date of this instrument." Royden Reliable is only authorized to negotiate and execute the contract for the property at 9876 Wainiha Street. He does not have any other powers, and everyone who deals with him is put on notice that his powers are valid only for three months.

Because the power of attorney is designed for use when the principal is unavailable to do certain things, the document must be drafted with clarity and certainty to avoid any question regarding the attorney-in-fact's authorization. Any question that delays the signing of the document defeats the very purpose for which the power of attorney was prepared.

Powers of attorney have been signed by spouses employed out of state for prolonged periods, granting the power of attorney to the spouse living in Hawaii. A husband might sign a special power of attorney authorizing his wife, residing in Hawaii, to sign a contract to sell their real property on his behalf. When an attorney-in-fact signs on behalf of a principal, she signs as follows:

Kenneth Kwajalein
by Katie Kwajalein, His Attorney-in-Fact

When the attorney-in-fact signs an instrument relating to real estate that is recorded in the Bureau of Conveyances, such as a deed or agreement of sale, the power of attorney must also be recorded to give full effect to the conveyance of the real estate. Without the recordation of the power of attorney, there is no notice to the world of the attorney-in-fact's power to act on behalf of the principal.

Hawaii has adopted the *durable power of attorney* concept in which the principal is permitted to create a power of attorney that continues despite the principal's later disability. Formerly, when the principal was incapacitated, the attorney-in-fact could no longer exercise any power granted to him or her under a power of attorney. Words to the effect that "this power of attorney shall not be affected by subsequent disability or incapacity of the principal" should be stated in the instrument. A power of attorney automatically becomes invalid upon the death of the principal.

IMPORTANT POINTS: In buying or selling real estate,

1. The person you are dealing with must be legally competent to enter into a contract.
2. If more than one person owns the property, all owners must sign the contract.
3. If a corporation is buying or selling the property, be sure to obtain a certificate of resolution authorizing the corporation to buy or sell.
4. In a partnership, only a general partner can sign on behalf of the partnership. A limited partner has no authority to sign on behalf of the partnership.
5. A trustee must sign a contract in the capacity of trustee when title to the property is in a trust.
6. In a guardianship, the ward or protected person holds title to the property, but the guardian has authority to act for the ward or the protected person. In the usual situation, the guardian obtains the necessary authorization from the court to sell or buy real estate.
7. The power-of-attorney document should be examined to find out the powers granted to the attorney-in-fact.

9 What Are the Essential Elements of a Contract to Purchase and Sell?

As the buyer or seller of real estate, you should know the basic requirements of a real estate contract to avoid legal problems and enter into a valid and binding agreement. A buyer who is likely to face legal problems is not only confronted with the possibility of litigation but may also have a financing problem. It may be difficult for such a buyer to obtain a loan to purchase a property, because lenders, like everyone else, do not want to be involved in lawsuits. The purpose of this chapter is to inform you of the essential elements that must be present in a contract to purchase and sell real estate in order for it to be enforceable.

First of all, the law known as the Statute of Frauds requires that any transaction involving real estate be in writing and be signed by the party against whom the contract is to be enforced.

EXAMPLE: Abel Adams and Cain Adams are brothers. Cain decides to sell his residence, and Abel agrees to buy it. Abel asks Cain, "Shouldn't we put our agreement in writing?" Cain gives the classic response, "Trust me. I'll sell it to you." Later, however, Cain refuses to sell. Abel cannot enforce the agreement against Cain because the agreement is not in writing.

Although there are exceptions to the requirement that the agreement be in writing, as when the person seeking enforcement has partially performed the contract in reliance upon the other party's representation to go through with the agreement, in almost all other instances it is necessary that there be a contract in writing containing the promises and understanding reached between the seller and the buyer.

Even a simple memorandum or note stating all of the important points of understanding signed by the party against whom the contract is to be enforced or someone authorized by that party is helpful evidence of the agreement reached between the seller and buyer. Most courts require the written memorandum to disclose (1) the identity of the parties, either by name or description; (2) identification of the property; (3) *consideration,* that is, the purchase price and terms of payment; and (4) in most jurisdictions, the signature of the person against whom the contract is to be enforced.

> EXAMPLE: Abel Adams and Cain Adams write a memo of their mutual oral promises with the understanding that their agreement is to be written into a formal contract: "I, Cain Adams, agree to sell my property located at 123 Church Street, Honolulu, Hawaii, to Abel Adams for $200,000 in cash." Both Able and Cain sign the memo. If Cain later refuses to sign the formal contract and go through with his oral promise to sell the property, Abel has the right to bring legal action against Cain based on the memo.

An oral contract is not void; it is simply unenforceable against the person to be charged with the contract, that is, the person who should perform the contract. In the usual situation, the plaintiff files a lawsuit to compel the defendant to perform his or her part of the bargain. As a defense against the plaintiff's claim, the defendant raises the issue of the Statute of Frauds. The purpose of the Statute of Frauds in requiring a real estate transaction to be put in writing is to produce certainty of the obligations of the parties to the contract and to remove the possibility of proving a nonexistent transaction by false testimony or perjury.

In the sale of real estate, as in the law of contracts generally, there must be a mutual assent by the parties to buy and to sell a certain real estate. More specifically, there must be an offer to purchase by the buyer and an acceptance of the offer by the seller to constitute mutual assent on the part of both parties. The customary practice in Hawaii is to have the buyer tender to the seller a contract referred to as the Deposit Receipt, Offer, and Acceptance (DROA), on the form by that name printed by the Board of Realtors (see appendix C). If the seller accepts all of the terms and conditions of the buyer by signing the DROA, a valid, enforceable contract is formed. If the seller makes a counter-offer, the standard Counter Offer form (appendix C) is signed by both parties and attached to the DROA.

Even if a written agreement has been signed by both the seller and the buyer, the basic and essential terms and conditions, proposed by the buyer in the DROA or by the seller in a counter-offer and accepted by the buyer, must be reasonably certain. If the terms and conditions of the contract are indefinite, the contract can be voided. It is the rule of law that the more indefinite the terms of a contract, the less likely it is that the parties intended to enter into a contract. The contract must be sufficiently explicit so that the court can perceive the rights and obligations of the parties.

A contract to purchase and sell real estate should include the following material information and must be signed by the seller and the buyer.

Property description. The property to be sold must be sufficiently described in the contract to be identifiable. It is the usual practice to indicate the street address and the apartment number, if applicable, and the *tax map key number* of the real estate being sold. All real estate in Hawaii has a tax map key number. If you, as the property owner, are unsure of the tax map key number, you can find it in the tax maps in the tax map section of the county real estate tax assessment office. If the property to be sold is a condominium apartment, it too will have a tax map key number. It is not necessary to give the *legal description* of the property in the DROA. In other words, the metes and bounds description or the land court description is not usually stated in the DROA. (An explanation of the legal description of real estate is covered in chapter 11.)

Price and terms of payment. Another important element of a real estate contract, price, is probably the most important element in the contract, because unless the price is mutually agreed upon by the seller and buyer, the chances of forming a contract are negligible. Most real estate negotiation involves the price of the property to be sold. In a seller's market there is a great demand for real estate and an insufficient supply. In a buyer's market, in which there is an oversupply of real estate and less demand, the buyer has greater negotiating power with respect to the price of the property.

The buyer who is not able to pay cash for the entire purchase price of the property has an obligation to describe how the purchase price is to be paid. The contract must indicate the *terms of payment,* that is, how the buyer will finance the purchase of the property. The numerous ways of financing the purchase will be discussed in greater detail in the next chapter. If the method of financing is not clearly stated, the contract will be interpreted to mean that the buyer intends to pay the entire price in cash at the closing of the transaction. If the purchase is financed through a mortgage, the contract will explicitly state:

Purchase price	$300,000	
Down payment	$100,000	in cash
Balance	$200,000	by way of a mortgage, 10.5% annual interest, 30 years term

In the above illustration, unless the buyer obtains a mortgage at an annual interest rate of 10.5 percent and for a term of thirty years, the offer to purchase is deemed to be cancellable by the buyer. The specification of financing terms indicates to the seller the way the buyer intends to pay for the property.

Closing date. Every contract must set a date on which the deal *closes.* This is the date by which all required documents must be signed by the parties and recorded at the Bureau of Conveyances. In most situations, the closing is handled by an escrow (the role of the escrow is discussed in chapter 13). The seller will sign the conveyance instrument transferring interest in the property to the buyer, and the buyer, in turn, will take all necessary steps to pay the purchase price. If the purchase is to be financed through a financial institution, the loan documents are usually signed by the buyer before the closing. The payment of the cash or loan funds to the seller is handled by the escrow. Under current local practice, payment is made after the conveyance instruments are recorded at the Bureau of Conveyances. The actual payment of the cash or funds is made after checking the title to the property by the escrow. If, at the time of recordation, the escrow finds a *lien* (claim) not recorded earlier, the escrow notifies both parties, because most transactions are conditioned on the property being sold free and clear of liens. Checking the title at the time of recordation protects the buyer, because if after the funds were transferred the seller could not be located or could not pay the lien, the buyer would end up being responsible for paying the lien on the property just purchased. Checking title at recordation is one of the important services performed by the escrow.

Broker's commission. A provision in the contract that involves the seller but not the buyer is the seller's agreement to pay a commission to his or her broker. In the contract, the seller instructs the escrow to pay the commission directly to the broker at closing. The seller also gives permission to his broker to share the commission with the broker who represents the buyer and is named in the contract.

Evidence of good title. In all contracts for the acquisition of real property, the buyer should require the seller to furnish at closing evidence of *marketable title* of the real property from a licensed abstractor or title company. When the seller agrees to furnish evidence of marketable title, then he or she must obtain a document from a title company showing that the seller has a marketable title to the property on or by the closing date. In the usual case, if the seller is unable to deliver a marketable title, the buyer has the option of cancelling the contract and having all monies that the buyer has paid refunded. A buyer whose title to real property is under a cloud may have difficulty reselling the property later, because no one wants to purchase property with a defect in the title. Moreover, a title insurance company may decline to insure the title for a subsequent buyer. Lastly, no reputable financial institution will make a loan on a property with a defect in the title. In a purchase involving a sizable investment, it is a good practice for the buyer to obtain the title report before signing the contract, or at least before closing and have an attorney review it.

> IMPORTANT POINT: In the purchase and sale of residential real estate in Hawaii, a printed form called the Deposit Receipt, Offer, and Acceptance (DROA) is used in almost all instances. You might think it an easy task simply to fill in the relevant information. If the information is erroneous or the form is incomplete, however, the contract may be deemed invalid and unenforceable. Therefore, it is extremely important that you, as either the seller or the buyer, read the contract carefully to be sure that all of the essential information is accurately inserted on the DROA. Never be too embarrassed to ask your broker if there is any question in your mind. Although you may not be an expert, your common sense may tell you when something is not quite right.

REFERENCE: Limitation of Action. Chapter 656, *Hawaii Revised Statutes*.

10 How Should You Finance the Purchase of the Property?

MORTGAGE UPDATE

1-MONTH ADJUSTABLE RATE MORTGAGE

SIMPLE INTEREST | ESTIMATED ANNUAL PERCENTAGE RATE | Based on a
7.50% | **10.28%** |

1-YEAR ADJUSTABLE RATE MO

SIMPLE INTEREST | ESTIMATED ANNUAL PERCENTAGE RATE |
8.50% | **10.29%** |

15-YEAR FIXED RATE SECOND M(

SIMPLE INTEREST | ESTIMATED ANNUAL PERCENTAGE RATE |
10.75% | **11.11%** |

BANK

THIS NOTE IS LEGAL TENDER
FOR ALL DEBTS, PUBLIC AND PRIVATE

A 08643556 E

WASHINGTON, D.C.

Even before you decide to purchase a particular property—for exam-ple, a house and lot on Anania Drive in Mililani—you should be thinking about how to pay for the property. Consider the different ways of financing the purchase at the same time you look at proper-ties. Paying for a property is no problem if you have the cash to pay the entire purchase price. In most instances, however, purchasers will not have enough cash to pay the entire purchase price. Even if you do have enough cash, you may still consider financing a portion of the purchase price, because you may wish to retain some of the cash for emergency purposes, education, home improvement, or other reasons. Moreover, in instances when the property is to be your residence or your first vacation home, the interest on the loan may still be deducted for income tax purposes under the Tax Reform Act and is a form of a tax shelter.

It is important to understand the ways of financing the purchase of your home, because unless you have the cash to purchase the home, you will have no alternative but to obtain financing. The customary ways of financing the purchase of residential real property in Hawaii are discussed below.

Mortgage

A *mortgage* is a conveyance of real property by the borrower to the lender to secure the repayment of a debt. If the debt is not repaid as agreed upon by the borrower, the lender can compel the sale of the real property and apply the proceeds of the sale toward the repayment of the debt. The lender takes title to the property as a *collateral,* a property given as security for the performance of the borrower's promise to pay the loan.

> EXAMPLE: Jon and Ann Homeseekers enter into a contract to purchase a house and lot on Anania Drive in Mililani for $200,000 of which $50,000 will be paid in cash. The balance of $150,000 will be paid by way of a mortgage. The lender is First United Mortgage Corp., which is the *mortgagee*. Jon and Ann, who are the borrowers, are called the *mortgagors*. The collateral is the house and lot on Anania Drive, Mililani.
>
> In a mortgage loan, the borrower signs two documents, the promissory note and the mortgage document. Both are contracts.

Promissory Note

A valid promissory note (sometimes simply referred to as a "note") must be in writing and contain, among other features, the following important elements: the name and address of the borrower (known as the *maker*) and the lender (known as the *holder*); the borrower's promise to pay a certain sum of money (the amount of the loan), which is referred to as the *principal;* the interest rate; the terms of repayment, for example, the amount of a monthly payment, when the monthly payments are due, and the number of monthly payments; and the signature of the borrower. If the note is secured by a mortgage, it must state "this note is secured by a mortgage." Otherwise it is simply considered a personal obligation of the borrower.

A note may also contain a prepayment privilege, allowing the borrower to pay more than the required monthly payment or to pay the loan off earlier than required without payment of any penalty. Some lenders, in order to be assured of earning interest at a certain rate for a certain period of time, will insert a penalty clause in the promissory note, allowing the lender to assess a penalty if the borrower pays off the loan earlier than agreed upon by the borrower.

A note will almost always contain an *acceleration clause* allowing the lender to demand immediate payment of the entire principal balance remaining on the note when the borrower becomes delinquent in making any payment. It is customary, however, for the lender to allow the borrower a *grace period* to accommodate late payments. If the due date of the monthly payment falls on the first day of each month, for example, the lender may give the borrower a ten-day grace period for any late payment. The note will usually also provide that if any payment is made after the grace period, a late charge of a certain amount or certain percentage of the monthly payment may be charged against the borrower. The borrower will also promise to pay any collection costs, including reasonable attorney's fees and costs, incurred by the lender in taking action against the borrower for late payments or other contractual obligations.

If two or more persons sign the note, it will generally state that the borrowers are "jointly and severally liable" for all obligations that the borrowers agree to perform in the note, meaning that the borrowers are liable as a group and individually for the entire loan.

> EXAMPLE: If Gail Goldenpurse and Bart Rottenguy both sign a note and Bart skips town one step ahead of his creditors, the lender has the right to pursue only Gail for payment of the entire loan. The lender is not obligated to go after both Gail and Bart. More important, the lender, after obtaining a judgment against Gail and Bart, may recover entirely from Gail's assets.

Mortgage Document

Whereas the note is evidence of a debt and a promise to pay the debt by the borrower, the mortgage is the document in which the borrower transfers real estate to the lender as collateral to reassure the payment of a debt. The key provisions commonly found in a mortgage are summarized below.

The mortgage document will contain the names of the borrower (mortgagor) and the lender (mortgagee), the date of the document, and the amount of the debt, which is the loan amount. It will include specific language whereby the borrower conveys to the lender real property, which is the collateral for the loan. Generally but not always, it will be the property being purchased with the loan money. In Hawaii, the transfer of title simply gives the lender a *lien right;* the borrower is allowed to remain on the property and retains *beneficial ownership,* which is all rights and privileges enjoyed by the owners of real estate. The lender, however, possesses the right to *foreclose* on the mortgage if the borrower fails to live up to the terms and conditions of the mortgage. To foreclose on a mortgage means to terminate the rights of the mortgagor in the mortgaged property. The property is then absolutely owned by the mortgagee, who can sell the property for payment of the debt.

In the mortgage document, the borrower *warrants* (guarantees) to the lender that the property being mortgaged is the borrower's property and will be defended against ownership claims made by others. In order to protect the lender's interest in the mortgaged property, the mortgage will also contain several *covenants* (promises) by the borrower, such as covenants to pay real property taxes, obtain insurance against damage or destruction, and keep the property in good repair. The document may also contain a *due on sale clause,* similar to the acceleration provision in the note, giving the lender the right to call the loan in case of any breach of the mortgage agreement by the borrower. It allows the lender to terminate the loan and demand immediate payment in full of the loan balance. If the borrower is unable to pay the balance, the lender has the right to foreclose the property and sell it. When interest rates were high, the due on sale clause was used by lenders to eliminate old loans with low interest rates.

When a loan is paid off, the lender will cancel the note and prepare a *release of mortgage,* stating that the note is paid in full and the mortgage is satisfied and has been discharged. It is very important that the borrower record the release of mortgage at the Bureau of Conveyances. Otherwise, the public records will continue to show the property to be encumbered with the mortgage. The borrower should request the mortgage release from the lender and record it promptly.

Loan Points

When a lender refers to "points" in discussing the cost of obtaining a loan, one point is equal to one percent of the loan amount. Thus, for example, two points in a $100,000 loan is $2,000 ($100,000 × .02 = $2,000).

Points are usually discussed in the context of *loan origination fees* and sometimes with reference to a change sought by the lender in the effective yield of a mortgage loan. The purpose of the loan origination fee is to cover the lender's costs and expenses in making the loan to the borrower, including the time and effort spent by a loan officer of the lending institution in processing the loan and reviewing the loan documents, the office overhead, and other functions necessary to complete the loan. In essence, it is the fee the borrower pays to obtain a loan. It is separate and apart from the interest the borrower pays on the loan amount.

Discount points are points charged by the lender to raise the lender's return on the loan. The financial institution makes a profit in its lending business by charging interest. A lender can make a further profit with charges other than interest, for instance, discount points.

EXAMPLE: On a $1,000 loan with interest at 10 percent per annum payable in one year, the borrower pays $1,100 at the end of one year ($1,000 × .10 = $100; $1,000 + $100 = $1,100). The effective yield on the loan is 10 percent. However, if the borrower receives only $900 rather than the full $1,000 from the lender at the time of the loan, the borrower has been charged $100 for the loan. The lender still requires the borrower to pay the principal of $1,000 and a 10 percent per annum interest of $100 at the end of the year. The charge of $100 is a discount point, which the borrower pays from the loan amount. This charge raises the yield to the lender without raising the interest rate on the loan, since the lender under this loan procedure is repaid $200 on the loan.

$$\$1,000 - \$900 = \$100 \text{ (discount point)}$$
$$\underline{+100 \text{ (interest)}}$$
$$\text{Total} \quad \$200$$

Discount points are generally charged during tight money periods when mortgage money is in short supply.

FHA and VA Loans

In 1934, Congress enacted the National Housing Act, one provision of which established the Federal Housing Administration (FHA) to encourage new construction of homes in the hope of creating jobs. The FHA was to accomplish this construction by insuring lending institutions against losses due to nonpayment by borrowers on loans made to them on new and existing homes. In return, lenders had to grant long-term loans, for twenty years or more, in contrast to the three- to five-year loans common at the time. Furthermore, lenders had to raise the *loan-to-value ratio* from 50 or 60 percent to as much as 80 percent. The loan-to-value ratio is the ratio between the loan a lender is willing to make to a borrower and the lender's estimate of the fair market value of the property that is to be pledged as security.

> EXAMPLE: A buyer desires to purchase a residence offered for sale at $200,000. The lender has it appraised and learns that the fair market value as appraised is also $200,000. The lender agrees to make a loan of 80 percent loan-to-value, which is 80 percent of $200,000, or $160,000. The remaining $40,000 must be paid in cash by the borrower.

The FHA inspects the property to be certain that it meets the construction quality acceptable to the FHA and to determine the fair market value. It also charges the borrower an insurance fee, which is a percentage of the loan balance. The ceiling on the amount insured by FHA changes as the fair market value of properties increase.

The borrower receiving an FHA loan may not obtain a second mortgage on the same property to raise down payment funds. The FHA requires that the borrower bring in some cash toward the purchase price. A significant change brought about by the FHA is the loan application review system in which the borrower's earning power is considered in addition to his assets. When the law was first enacted, emphasis was placed on the borrower's assets rather than ability to meet the monthly mortgage payments.

When applying for a loan at the bank, you should inquire whether an FHA loan is available for the residence you are purchasing. If it is available, you should compare whether such a loan is advantageous for you. Because you are required to pay the FHA insurance fee at closing, you will pay more at closing than on a conventional loan. But the interest rate for an FHA loan is often lower than for a conventional loan.

The loan commonly referred to as a VA (Veterans Administration) loan, like the FHA loan, is a loan guaranteed by the federal government. The VA loan was part of the package of benefits extended to World War II veterans, which included aid in education, hospitalization, employment training, and housing. In the area of housing, the federal government was empowered to guarantee the repayment of a portion of the first mortgage loans made to veterans. In return for the guarantee, the lender would not charge the veteran any fees to make a loan. In the law originally enacted in 1944, the lender was guaranteed against losses up to 50 percent of the loan but not greater than $2,000 (the cost of residential real property was significantly lower in those days).

The law was passed with the objective of enabling veterans to purchase a home without having to make a cash down payment. The $2,000 loan guarantee to the lender was like a down payment by the veteran, for if the veteran were to default on the loan and the property was foreclosed, the lender could look to the federal government for payment of the $2,000, and the balance of the loan would come from the sale proceeds of the property.

VA loans are administered by the Veterans Administration. For a long time, the guarantee was 100 percent of the first $27,500 and 95 percent above that amount, not to exceed $90,000. However, the guarantee has gone up during the past several years. Many financial institutions will lend more than the maximum amount if the veteran makes a down payment and has enough income to support the monthly mortgage payments.

All veterans and active duty military personnel are eligible for a VA loan. Spouses of veterans who died as a result of military service can also obtain housing guarantees if they are not remarried. In order to obtain a VA loan, the veteran must first apply for a certificate of eligibility, which gives evidence of the veteran's qualification and the amount of guarantee available. Lenders will require the certificate before processing a VA loan.

In order to protect the veteran, the Veterans Administration will have the property to be purchased by the veteran appraised and will issue a *certificate of reasonable value* (CRV), informing the veteran of the appraised value and the maximum VA guaranteed loan a lender may make on the property. The VA will guarantee the loan on a home for thirty years.

With a VA loan, unlike an FHA loan, the veteran is liable in the case of a mortgage foreclosure if a loss is sustained by the VA. In the case of an FHA loan, the borrower pays a fee for protection against any foreclosure losses.

The eligibility and benefits under the VA loan program are frequently changed by Congress. Therefore, a veteran applying for a VA loan should inquire with the local VA office to learn the up-to-date requirements and benefits.

Truth in Lending Act

The Federal Consumer Credit Protection Act, popularly referred to as the Truth in Lending Act, was enacted by Congress in 1969. The Act as implemented by the Federal Reserve Board's Regulation Z requires a lender to clearly show the borrower how much he or she is paying for credit in terms of dollars and as a percentage before he or she becomes committed to the loan. The borrower has the right to rescind (cancel) the loan agreement in certain instances. The purpose of the law is to enable borrowers to compare the various credit terms available by establishing a standard by which the credit terms can be measured.

The law requires the lender to disclose the terms and conditions of the loan in writing to the borrower before the borrower commits himself to the loan contact. So that the borrower will know the annual cost of credit, the lender must apply a uniform measure called the *annual percentage rate* (APR). This rate includes the interest rate, loan fees, discount points, and any other costs that contribute to the true annual cost of borrowing from the lender. All of these costs must be shown together in a single figure. The lender is also required to disclose the *total finance charge,* which is the total of all costs the borrower must pay for obtaining credit. This charge includes discount points, loan fees, loan service fees, required life insurance, and interest.

Under the Truth in Lending Act, borrowers generally have the right to rescind a loan contract within three business days after it is signed.

Purchase Money Mortgage

Often the seller of real property will accept payment of part of the purchase price with a note and mortgage from the buyer. In other words, the seller finances part of the sale of her property, and the buyer avoids the necessity of applying for a loan from a financial institution for the money needed for the balance of the purchase price.

> EXAMPLE: The purchase price of a condominium is $200,000. The buyer pays a down payment of $25,000 and is only able to obtain a first mortgage of $150,000, leaving a balance of $25,000. The seller may agree to accept a *purchase money mortgage* for the $25,000. In this situation, the purchase money mortgage is also a *second mortgage.*

Agreement of Sale

In a true sense, an agreement of sale is not a way of financing the purchase of real property. Under the Hawaii statute, an agreement of sale is defined as "an executory contract for the sale and purchase of real estate which binds one party to sell and the other party to buy real estate which is the subject matter of the transaction, and in which the seller retains legal title to the real estate."[3]

An *executory contract* is a contract in which there are certain terms and conditions that need to be performed by one of the parties to the contract or both. In one of the first agreement-of-sale cases that came before the Hawaii Supreme Court, the court described an agreement of sale as follows:

"An agreement of sale in this jurisdiction has become a common and established device utilized in the sale and purchase of real property. It is an executory contract which binds the vendor [seller] to sell and the vendee [purchaser] to buy the realty which constitutes the subject matter of the transaction. . . . It is often the only means by which low income purchasers are able to buy land, for the agreement of sale transaction enables them, initially at least, to bypass the substantial down payment requirements based on a loan-to-value ratios imposed upon lending institutions for conventional loans by state and federal regulations. The vendor, on the other hand, can establish his own ratios and thus is able to effect an enlargement of the land and housing market towards which his sales efforts are directed."[4]

The Supreme Court also indicated that under an agreement of sale the legal title to the property remains in the seller's name, while the *equitable (and beneficial) ownership* vests in the buyer, and, unless the agreement provides otherwise, the buyer is entitled to immediate possession of the property. The court pointed out that legal title is retained by the seller essentially as security for payment of the purchase price by the buyer. The agreement also provides for cancellation and forfeiture, at the seller's option, in case of default by the buyer in payment of the purchase price.

There are two important advantages for the buyer purchasing under an agreement of sale: (1) The buyer is able to set a purchase price for the property, with a balance, commonly referred to as the *balloon payment,* to be paid in full at an agreed upon date in the future. This practice is particularly advantageous in an inflationary market when the prices accelerate at a rapid rate. The maturity date, when the full purchase price must be paid, may be any time from six months to five years after the agreement is signed, or even later. However, once the purchase price has been set, the seller is unable to raise it in the future; (2) The buyer need not obtain financing from a financial institution when he or she enters into the agreement of sale, thus avoiding all the complications and paperwork involved in bank financing of a home. Generally, the buyer will make a down payment toward the purchase price and agree to pay interest on the principal balance for a predetermined period of time.

EXAMPLE: Karen Kala, owner of a condominium unit in the Kaanapali Waves, enters into an agreement of sale to sell the unit to rock singer Prince Jackson for $1,000,000, with a $250,000 down payment, the balance to be paid in three years with interest at the rate of 10 percent per annum on the unpaid balance. In this case, Prince Jackson will pay 10 percent interest on the balance of $750,000, or $75,000 a year, for three years. At the end of three years, Prince Jackson is obligated to pay the balance of $750,000. In this situation, Karen Kala, having agreed to sell the condominium for $1,000,000, cannot change the price no matter how much the value has increased.

Trust Deed

The *trust deed,* or deed of trust, is not commonly used in Hawaii. However, many Hawaii residents purchase real estate in other states, such as California, where the deed of trust is used. A trust deed is the same as a mortgage in that real estate is used as collateral for a loan and if the loan is not repaid as agreed upon by the borrower, the property is foreclosed and sold and the proceeds are applied to the loan balance.

In a transaction involving a mortgage, there are two parties: the mortgagee, who is the lender, and the mortgagor, who is the borrower. When a trust deed is used, there are three parties to the loan transaction: the trustor, who is the borrower; the beneficiary, who is the lender; and the trustee, who is a neutral third party. In a trust deed loan, the lender makes a loan to the borrower, who signs and delivers a note and a trust deed to the lender. In the trust deed instrument, the borrower conveys title to the trustee rather than to the lender. The trust deed is recorded where the property is located, and it is held by the lender for safekeeping until the note is paid.

When the loan is paid in full, the lender forwards to the trustee the note, the trust deed, and a request for reconveyance. The trustee then cancels the note and issues a *reconveyance deed* or *release deed,* which transfers the title back to the borrower. Like the release of mortgage, the reconveyance deed should be recorded in the jurisdiction where the property is located to give notice to the world that the borrower now holds title unencumbered by a loan.

If the borrower defaults under the note, the lender delivers the trust deed to the trustee with instructions to sell the property and pay the loan balance to the lender. The sale can be accomplished by the trustee, because the borrower has already conveyed title to the trustee. In addition, the trust deed contains a power of sale empowering the trustee to sell the property without the necessity of a court foreclosure proceeding.

Interest Rates and Usury

When the buyer borrows money to purchase real estate, the lender will charge interest on the amount of money borrowed. The lender is not free to charge whatever rate of interest the market will bear, since interest rates are regulated by statute.

Whenever there is a written contract between a lender and a borrower, they may agree to an interest rate not to exceed 1 percent per month, which is 12 percent per year, and the borrower must sign such a contract. If there is no express written contract fixing the rate of interest, the interest shall be charged at the rate of 10 percent per year.

Usury refers to an interest rate higher than that permitted by law. A contract charging a usurious rate is not void, but, in a legal action in which the lender is plaintiff, if proof is made that a greater rate of interest than 1 percent per month has been directly or indirectly contracted for, the plaintiff recovers only the principal and the defendant recovers cost of the law suit. No legal action may be filed to recover compound interest in any contract whatever.

If the lender is a bank, however, and this is very important, the bank may charge, contract for, receive, collect in advance, or recover interest, discount, and other charges at the same rates and in the same amounts permitted by law of loans made by industrial loan companies, which generally charge a higher interest rate. There are certain other exemptions to usury. The exemptions that are relevant to the subject of this book are

1. A mortgage loan wholly or partially secured by a guarantee, insurance, or a commitment to insure involving the FHA or the VA.

2. A loan secured by a first mortgage lien on real property or a first lien on stock in a residential cooperative housing corporation that was agreed to or incurred after May 30, 1980.

3. An agreement of sale made after May 30, 1980, under which a seller agrees to sell real property to a buyer but retains legal title to the real property and in which the rate of interest is clearly stated. However, in any extension at maturity or renegotiation of such an agreement of sale made on or after July 1, 1985, the maximum rate of interest charged cannot be more than four percentage points above the weekly average yield on United States Treasury securities adjusted to a constant maturity of three years, as made available by the Federal Reserve Board at the time of extension or renegotiation. The agreement of sale includes any subagreement of sale or subsequent subagreement of sale made on or after June 18, 1982.

4. A loan secured by a purchase-money junior mortgage on real property that is agreed to and incurred after June 18, 1982.

5. A loan made by an employee welfare benefit trust plan or an employee pension benefit plan approved by the Internal Revenue Service and the United States Department of Labor[5] or a loan made by the employees' retirement system of the State of Hawaii.

Thus, under the exceptions to the usury law, there are many loans in which the interest rate may exceed the annual rate of 12 percent. When applying for a loan, if the interest rate exceeds 12 percent, be sure the loan falls under one of the exceptions to the law.

REFERENCES: *Usury.* Chapter 478, *Hawaii Revised Statutes.* National Housing Act. Chapter 13, Title 12, *United States Code.* Veterans Benefits Act. Subchapters I and II, Chapter 37, Title 38, *United States Code.*

There are other important matters that must be taken into account in obtaining a loan, such as the criteria in qualifying for a loan and the financial institutions at which to apply for a loan. Each financial institution sets its own conditions and standards to qualify for a loan. Applying for a loan requires that you complete many forms and sign many documents.

> IMPORTANT POINT: In the process of seeking a loan, your real estate broker should prove to be of great assistance to you. Some real estate brokers maintain the current interest rates of various financial institutions, thereby reducing the time you spend shopping around for the best interest rate. You should be thinking of financing your home purchase as soon as you seriously consider purchasing a home.

11 Do You Have Good Title to Your Property?

A person purchasing real estate should obtain from the seller good title of the property. The technical term for good title is *marketable title*. *Title* in the context of real estate refers to ownership of a property. In a Hawaii case, the Hawaii Supreme Court in defining marketable title stated that it is a title free from litigation, palpable defects, and grave doubts. "It signifies a title as to which there is no doubt, either at law or in fact, as will affect the market value."[6]

Abstract and Title Report

As evidence of marketable title of the property being sold, the seller may deliver to the buyer at the time of closing an *abstract* of the property, which is a complete historical summary of all recorded instruments and documents affecting the title to the property. The abstract is simply a report by a person (the abstractor) who conducted a search of the documents recorded at the Bureau of Conveyances, the Department of Commerce and Consumer Affairs, the

Department of Health, the courts, and any other public records affecting the property. The abstract sets forth the chain of title that links the title of the present owner to the first owner. Any break in the chain of recorded title may result in a finding that the title is not marketable.[7] An abstract showing the entire chain of title is expensive to prepare, and, therefore, it may simply contain the most recent transactions involving the property or be limited to transactions involving the present property owner.

As an alternative to an abstract, the seller may deliver a *title report* as evidence of his marketable title in the property. Delivery of a title report is the general practice in Hawaii. A title company renders an opinion regarding the owner of the property and lists all other parties who may have a right or interest in the property, such as mortgage lenders, lessees, or judgment creditors. Whereas an abstract is a summary of all recorded documents or information affecting the title to a property, a title report shows the condition of the title at a specific time, like a snapshot. It does not mention all previous property owners; it simply indicates the current owner. The title report also lists all present *encumbrances* (claims or liens on the property) affecting the property.

Contents of the Title Report

Legal Description

In the Deposit Receipt, Offer, and Acceptance Agreement (DROA), which is the agreement to purchase and sell real estate in Hawaii, the location of the property to be sold is designated by a street address and, if the transaction involves a condominium unit, the apartment number.

> EXAMPLE: Street address: 2333 Kapiolani Boulevard, Apt. No. 4321, Marco Polo, Honolulu, Hawaii.
> If there is no street or road address: Lot 193, Onomea Homesteads, Onomea, Hawaii.

However, the location of the property in the DROA is not a legal description. It is merely an informal reference to the property site. It does not give the exact location of the property, describe the boundaries of the property, or reveal any encumbrances affecting the property. In Hawaii, there are three methods commonly used to describe real property: (1) metes and bounds, (2) reference to Land Court information, and (3) file plan number.

Metes and bounds. In describing a parcel of land by metes and bounds, the surveyor plots the land from a designated monument, such as an iron pipe, and then describes the parcel by metes (distance) and bounds (direction) from the monument. Distance is measured in feet, usually to the nearest tenth or one-hundredth of a foot. Direction is shown in degrees (°), minutes ('), and seconds ("), example, 100° 58' 3". There are 360 degrees in a circle, 60 minutes in each degree, and 60 seconds in each minute.

Because the monument could later be destroyed or removed, it is referenced by a connection line to a nearby permanent reference mark established by the surveyor's office, such as "Government Survey Triangulation Station 'Rosebank.'" The corner where the survey begins is called the *point of beginning* or *point of commencement,* and the survey continues clockwise along the parcel's boundaries.

LEGAL DESCRIPTION OF PROPERTY

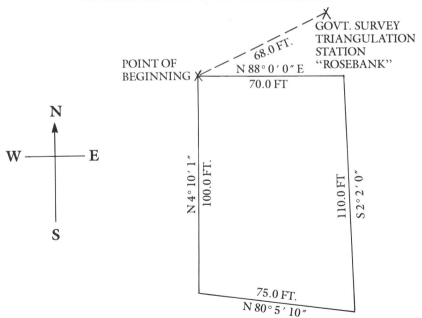

Land Court description. The metes and bounds description is commonly referred to as *regular system property.* Hawaii has also registered land based upon the Torrens system. Such land is referred to as *Land Court property* (a more comprehensive explanation of the Land Court system is found in chapter 16 of this book). The registration process is complex and costly, but one great advantage of Land Court property is that no one can acquire any right, title, or interest in the registered land by "prescription or adverse possession." In other words, a person squatting on another's property for twenty years continuously, exclusively, and hostilely, could not acquire right, title, or interest in the property.

The Land Court, before granting a decree of registration of title, requires a map of the land to be registered. The map must show all data necessary to enable the lines to be reproduced on the ground itself, and it must also contain or be accompanied by such data (such as survey lines from the surveyor's field notes) from enduring (permanent) monuments. Distances and functions of necessary angles must be shown definitely, not approximately. The legal description of Land Court property is designated by a lot number, application number, and the name of the original applicant.

> EXAMPLE: "All of that certain parcel of land situate at Kahaluu and Luukoi, District of Koolaupoko, City and County of Honolulu, State of Hawaii, described as follows:
>
>> Lot A-11, area 3.220 acres, as shown on Map 18, filed in the Office of the Assistant Registrar of the Land Court of the State of Hawaii with Land Court Application No. 2,000 of Kahaluu Land Company, Limited.
>
>> Being all of the land described in and covered by Transfer Certificate of Title No. 12345 issued to Kaneohe Bay Holdings, a Hawaii general partnership."

> REFERENCE: No Adverse Possession of Land Court Property. Section 501-87, *Hawaii Revised Statutes.*

File plan map. A third method of describing real property, known as the File Plan Map number, is used when a parcel of land is subdivided into several lots based upon the surveyor's file plan recorded in the Bureau of Conveyances. A metes and bounds survey would already have been plotted and a map prepared showing in detail the boundaries of each lot. Each lot would then have been assigned a number. Each subdivision tract is also assigned a number, and the File Plan Map, which is the subdivision map showing all the lots in the subdivision tract, is recorded in the Bureau of Conveyances. It is not necessary to describe each lot by metes and bounds. All that is necessary is a reference to the lot number and subdivision name.

> EXAMPLE: "All of that certain parcel of land situate at Kapahulu, Waikiki, City and County of Honolulu, State of Hawaii:
>
> Lot 2, area 15,000 square feet, in Block 14, as delineated on the map entitled Kaimuki Tract, which map having been filed in the Bureau of Conveyances of the State of Hawaii in Liber 178, at Page 294."

Easements

A title report may indicate that there is an easement affecting the property.

> EXAMPLE: "Grant of Easement in favor of The Hawaiian Electric Company, Limited, a Hawaii corporation, and Hawaiian Telephone Company, a Hawaii corporation, dated January 23, 1950, recorded in the Bureau of Conveyances in Liber 2220, at Page 100, granting a perpetual easement for utility purposes."
>
> EXAMPLE: "An easement of right-of-way to be used in common with others entitled thereto over Lots 10, 20, 30, and 40 being roadways, as shown on File Plan 999."

An *easement* is a right that one person has to use the land of another for a specific purpose. The easement is a burden on one property, the *servient,* for the benefit of another property, the *dominant.*

> EXAMPLE: Howard Homeowner owns a house and lot in Pearl City and grants a utility easement to The Hawaiian Electric Com-

pany, Ltd. Howard's property is now burdened by an easement in favor of Hawaiian Electric. His property is the servient property and Hawaiian Electric is the dominant property.

An easement is distinct from the right to occupy and enjoy the land itself. The easement owner has no title in the servient property but merely an interest in the servient land. An easement materially interferes with the full use or enjoyment of the servient land. Thus, in the example above, because Howard Homeowner's property is burdened with a utility easement in favor of The Hawaiian Electric Company, he will not have full use and enjoyment of his property.

Easements may be classified as affirmative or negative. An *affirmative easement* gives the owner of the dominant tenement (an interest in land) the right to use the servient tenement, for example, the right-of-way across another's land. A *negative easement* limits the freedom of a property owner to do what he pleases. Usually, negative easements are restrictions placed on all the lots in a subdivision to benefit all of the lot owners. Examples are building height restrictions, restrictions regarding the quality of building materials, and restrictions against blocking sunlight.

Most easements have been created by express grants of the previous land owner. Or, the grantor of a parcel of land can reserve (keep back, retain) an easement in the property.

EXAMPLE: "Reserving unto Mililani Sugar Company, Limited, a Hawaii corporation, its successors and assigns, all rights to underground waters and the right to construct, repair, and maintain such tunnels as said Mililani Sugar Company, Limited, may deem necessary for the development of such underground waters."

Occasionally, the property to be purchased may be subject to an *easement by necessity,* which may not be stated in the title report. An easement by necessity or *way of necessity* is an easement based on an *implied grant* and arises when a contiguous (neighboring) property is landlocked and shut off from access to a road. In such instances, an implied grant of way may exist for the landlocked property to use another property for purposes of ingress and egress.

In a Hawaii case referred to as the *Clarke* case, the sellers entered into a written contract with the purchasers whereby the sellers agreed to sell the property in question "free and clear of encumbrances." The purchasers visited the property twice before signing the contract, and on both occasions either the seller or her real estate salesperson was there to show the purchasers the property. Neither mentioned anything about the location of any structures extending beyond the boundary or the existence of a right-of-way running over and through a portion of the property in favor of other property owners. Only after the contract was signed and a down payment was made, and after the survey map was obtained, did the purchasers discover that the garage extended beyond the boundary line into the public road and that the residence encroached upon a right-of-way used by other property owners. The sellers refused to cancel the contract on the basis that because the easement or right-of-way was visible, the purchasers must be presumed to have had knowledge of its existence. The court in ruling for the purchasers stated:

> It is a well recognized rule, sustained by ample authority, that a contract to convey property, free and clear of encumbrances, is not complied with, where there exists an easement upon the land which precludes the full enjoyment of the premises. Numerous cases have held that even though an easement is comparatively a slight hindrance, yet it constitutes such a burden and impediment against the full enjoyment of the land as to affect merchantability and the purchaser is not obliged to accept the conveyance.

The *Clarke* case illustrates the importance of requiring the seller to deliver title to the property free and clear of all encumbrances.[8]

Encumbrance

An *encumbrance* is defined as a claim, lien, charge, or liability attached to and binding real property.

Some examples of encumbrances are mortgages, restrictions in a deed, the encroachment of a building upon the land of another, and leases. Another encumbrance is a *judgment lien,* a judgment obtained by one litigant, called the judgment creditor, against another, who is called the judgment debtor, that is recorded at the Bureau of Conveyances.

A *lien* is a claim that one person has upon the property of another on account of a debt owned by the property owner.

> EXAMPLE: Buster Blackhat owes money to Walter Whitehat. Blackhat fails to repay Whitehat, who files a court action against Blackhat and obtains a judgment. The judgment is recorded. Whitehat has a lien on the property owned by Blackhat.

It is a right that a creditor has in or over a property of a debtor as security for the debt. Only when the debt is paid in full is the lien discharged and the property free of the encumbrance.

> EXAMPLE: A judgment lien disclosed by the title report may indicate: "Judgment entered in favor of the plaintiff on January 3, 1987 in *Walter Whitehat v. Buster Blackhat,* in the Circuit Court of the Fifth Circuit, State of Hawaii, Civil No. 86-54321."

Any property owned by Blackhat is subject to the judgment lien, and, if and when any of Blackhat's property is sold, the net cash proceeds will first be paid to Whitehat to pay the judgment lien. If Land Court property is involved, a certified copy of the judgment should be delivered to the Assistant Registrar of the Land Court in order that the judgment may be noted on the owner's transfer certificate of title.

Another type of lien, which exists but is not often found on a title report, is a *mechanic's lien* or *materialman's lien*. These liens are claims created by law for the purpose of obtaining priority of payment of the price or value of work performed or materials furnished in the construction, renovation, or repair of a building or structure or improvements to land. Such a claim attaches to the land as well as to the building, structure, or improvement.

The person claiming a mechanic's lien or a materialman's lien (the *lienor*) is required to apply for the lien in the jurisdiction where the property is located. The application must be accompanied by a notice of a lien, which must be served upon the property owner and any person with an interest in the property and upon the parties who contracted for the improvements, if they are not the same as the property owner or person having an interest in the property. The application and notice must be filed not later than forty-five days after the completion of the improvements. The date of completion refers to the time when the owner or general contractor completes publication of a notice that the improvement has been completed or abandoned and files an affidavit of publication together with a copy of the notice with the clerk of the circuit court where the property is located.

A title report may disclose a *lis pendens*.

EXAMPLE: ". . . a lis pendens recorded in the Bureau of Conveyances on July 1, 1985, in *Clem Claimant v. Dexter Defendant,* in the Circuit Court of the Fifth Circuit, Civil No. 85-10001, in Liber 899999, at Page 2."

A lis pendens is a notice recorded in the Bureau of Conveyances or filed in the Land Court for the purpose of notifying all persons that title to a property is being litigated or that matters being litigated may relate to or involve the property. A person purchasing the property would be in danger of being bound by an adverse judgment. Therefore, if a lis pendens is mentioned on the title report, you, as the buyer, should inquire about the litigation. Failure to do so may result in your being saddled with a liability you did not intend to assume.

Another form of encumbrance that may affect a property is a *restrictive covenant* on the use of the land. A restrictive covenant is a covenant (agreement) that restricts or regulates the use of property or the kind, character, and location of buildings or other structures that may be constructed on the land.

EXAMPLE: "No commercial enterprise involving the keeping or raising of cattle, hogs, or other livestock will be maintained on the premises and no noxious industry will be permitted to be operated on said premises; that this covenant shall run with the land and jurisdiction may be taken in equity at the suit of the Grantor, its successors and assigns, and to restrain by injunction any violations or threatened violations of this covenant."

A common encumbrance in Hawaii is the following: "Reservation in favor of the State of Hawaii of all mineral and metallic mines." In most instances, the land owner is entitled to the property below the subsurface, but there is one exception in Hawaii. Minerals and metallic mines belong to the State of Hawaii. This encumbrance is accepted by all purchasers as a matter of course.

Frequently, a title report may simply state, for example, "The property is subject to the covenant relative to the use of said land as contained in Deed from Big Island Lehua Partners to Sam S. Samurai, dated November 1, 1950, recorded in Book 2587, Page 1000." Unless you were to read the deed itself, you would not know what the covenant involves. As a precaution, the prospective buyer should request a copy of the deed containing the covenant in order to determine the nature of the covenant.

This precaution also applies to condominium documents.

EXAMPLE: "The condominium apartment is subject to the covenants, agreements, obligations, conditions, and other provisions set forth in Declaration of Horizontal Property Regime, dated September 27, 1983, recorded on November 4, 1983, in Book 17435, at Page 648, and by the By-Laws recorded in Book 17435, at Page 679; as amended by Amendments recorded in Book 17435, at Page 685; as amended by Amendments recorded in Book 17484, at Page 94; Book 17752, at Page 587; Book 17967, at Page 170, and as same may hereafter be amended."

The buyer of a condominium apartment should read the Declaration of Horizontal Property Regime (now called the Declaration of Condominium Property Regime), the bylaws, and the amendments to determine what covenants, agreements, obligations, and conditions are contained in the documents before signing the contract to purchase the condominium apartment. It would be too late to request cancellation after the contract had been signed if you were to learn that some of the responsibilities of the apartment owner were burdensome and you did not wish to assume them.

REFERENCE: Mechanic's and Materialman's Lien. Part II, Chapter 507, *Hawaii Revised Statutes.*

Real Property Taxes

All title reports will disclose information concerning real property taxes on the property.

EXAMPLE:

TAXES FOR FISCAL YEAR 1990–1991 AND SUBSEQUENT YEARS

Tax key	: 4-7-14-876
Assessed value of land	: $100,000 (1990)
Exemption	: $0
Assessed value of improvements	: $150,000
Exemption	: $40,000
Net value	: $210,000

Taxes for the Fiscal Year 1990–1991 in the amount of $2,000 have been paid in full.

The information in the example indicates that the assessed value, placed on the property by the county real property tax assessor's office in 1990, for the land is $100,000, and the assessed value of the improvements to the property (including improvements to the dwelling structure, swimming pool, and so on) is $150,000, for a total of $250,000. The assessed value is based on information obtained by the assessor's office, generally from sales of real properties in the surrounding area. It is not necessarily the current fair market value that an appraiser would determine, because the information that the assessor obtains may not be up-to-date, particularly in a rapidly rising or falling real estate market. Still, the assessed value reflects 100 percent of the fair market value of the property. The tax rate is different for each county (real property taxes are discussed in chapter 18).

If payment of the real property taxes is current, the title report will show that the real property taxes have been paid in full. Delinquent taxes are also shown on the report. The prospective buyer should require the seller to pay any such delinquent taxes prior to the closing of the transaction or, at the latest, at the closing. If the seller fails to pay, the buyer will be responsible for the delinquent real property taxes.

> IMPORTANT POINT: The information contained in the title report provides the buyer with enough information to determine whether good title is being conveyed by the seller. If you are purchasing real estate and there is any question or doubt in your mind, you should delve more deeply or obtain more information to be satisfied that there is no cloud on the title that might adversely affect the marketable title of the property. Not all encumbrances will cause a cloud on the title. To determine to what extent an encumbrance might adversely affect the title, it is best to consult an attorney.

12 Are There Special Precautions in Acquiring Shoreline Properties?

When acquiring shoreline properties, there are precautions to be taken that are not necessary for inland properties. These precautions are significant enough that they could affect your decision to purchase a shoreline property. The first major difference between shoreline and inland properties is the setback of the seaward boundary. The second concerns legal restrictions imposed on any construction or improvement you may be contemplating on the water, such as a boat dock.

Shoreline Setback

Shoreline properties in Hawaii face a legal issue not involved in other properties. The question of how much of the shoreline belongs to the property owner and how much belongs to the public is still unresolved. This question has been litigated in both the state and federal courts, and the decisions of the courts have not been consistent. Ordinarily, the public has no legal right to use any portion of a land owner's property without the land owner's consent, and any person crossing or occupying another's property, even momentarily, is guilty of trespass. This prohibition does not necessarily apply to shoreline properties, as several legal cases illustrate.

In 1968, the Hawaii Supreme Court in determining the location of the seaward boundary dividing the private property and the public beach held that "the boundary is along the upper reaches of the wash of waves, usually evidenced by the edge of vegetation or by the line of debris left by the wash of waves."[9] Then, in 1973, the court stated:

> We hold as a matter of law that where the wash of the waves is marked by both a debris line and a vegetation line lying further mauka; the presumption is that the upper reaches of the wash of the waves over the course of a year lies along the line marking the edge of vegetation growth. The upper reaches of the wash of the waves at high tide during one season of the year may be further mauka than the upper reaches of the wash of the waves at high tide during the other seasons. Thus while the debris line may change from day to day or from season to season, the vegetation line is a more permanent monument, its growth limited by the year's highest wash of the waves.[10]

Thus, the Hawaii Supreme Court established the seaward boundary to be the vegetation line, which is farther inland than the debris line. The court also held that the land below the high-water mark is a natural resource owned by the state "subject to, but in some sense in trust for, the enjoyment of certain public rights." The court gave "judicial recognition of long-standing public use of Hawaii's beaches to an easily recognizable boundary that has ripened into a customary right." By the *Sotomura* decision, the right of a land owner to his or her property was diminished as the seaward boundary was set at the vegetation line, which is farther inland than the debris line.

Then, subsequently in 1978, the Federal District Court held:

> This Court fails to find any legal, historical, factual or other precedent or basis for the conclusions of the Hawaii Supreme Court that, following erosion, the monument by which the seaward boundary of seashore land in Hawaii is to be fixed is the upper reaches of the wash of the

waves. To the contrary, the evidence introduced in this case firmly establishes that the common law, followed by both legal precedent and historical practice, fixes the high water mark and seaward boundaries with
reference to the tides, as opposed to the run or reach of waves on the
shore.[11]

In reaching its decision, the court also stated:

Locating the high water mark by using the seaweed line was consistent
with accepted practice at the time and consistent with instructions to
the State (formerly Territorial) Surveyor contained in formal opinion of
the State (formerly Territorial) Attorney General. These instructions
were that high water mark was to be located, consistent with the common law, by reference to the tides and, more specifically, at or near the
level of the average of all of the high tides. . . .

The use of mean high water, or the seaweed line as its substantial equivalent, to locate high water mark on the ground was also in conformance
with the common law, adopted by §1–1, *Hawaii Revised Statutes,* as the
law of Hawaii. The common law defined high water mark by reference
to the elevations of the tides, disregarding the effect of wind and waves.
While there were differences of opinion as to which of the various high
tides fixed the high water mark, it was the tides, and not other criteria,
which at common law determined the location of high water mark.
Many cases expressly rejected physical marks made by the waters on the
shore and the extent of the run or reach of the waves on the shore.

Thus, the Federal District Court found the seaward boundary to be
the seaweed line, which is closer to the water than the vegetation
line.

The difference in opinion between the state and federal courts
still exists. As it stands, since the state decision fixes the seaward
boundary farther inland, along the edge of the vegetation growth,
the public is entitled to use more of the owners' properties as
opposed to the federal decision in which the seaward boundary is set
at the seaweed line, which is nearer the sea. This unsettled issue will
probably require another court decision or more cases before it will
be resolved. Until then, the owner of a shoreline property does not
know with certainty the seaward boundary of his or her seashore
property.

Construction and Regulations

In 1977, the state legislature established a Coastal Zone Management Program.[12] Earlier, in 1972, Congress had enacted the Federal Coastal Zone Management Act to encourage states in coastal areas to plan, manage, and regulate coastal lands. The law created a management and regulatory framework and appropriated federal funds to develop and implement state-run coastal zone management programs.

Under the Hawaii statute, the state retains overall power and control of the coastal lands to ensure that the development of such land is carried out in accordance with the state program. The counties are authorized to define special management areas (SMA) and to pass appropriate ordinances and regulations controlling the use of land within the county boundaries. The Hawaii statute requires that in carrying out the objectives of the coastal zone management program full consideration is given to "ecological, cultural, historic, and esthetic values as well as to needs for economic development."

The construction of single-family residences that are not part of a larger development or repairs, maintenance, or interior alterations to existing structures are excluded from county control of development in the coastal zone management area. Nor does it control the subdivision of land into lots greater than twenty acres or the subdivison of a parcel of land into four or fewer parcels when no associated construction activities are proposed.

Corps of Engineers

In the ordinary situation, all that is required to make an improvement to your property by constructing any type of structure, is a building permit issued by the county building department. If the plans and specifications of the structure meet the building and zoning code requirements, a building permit is issued. It is a relatively simple procedure. However, if your property is located along the shoreline or on water deemed to be either navigable or United States waters, there are stringent regulations involving several federal, state, and county authorities with which you must comply before you are permitted to make the improvement.

Any person, firm, or government agency (federal, state, or local) who plans to do any work in navigable or United States waters must obtain a permit from the U.S. Army Corps of Engineers. Examples of navigable and United States waters are ocean waters; coastal and inland waters, lakes, rivers, and streams, including adjacent wetlands; and fishponds connected to navigable waters. The following types of work may require a permit from the Corps of Engineers: (1) the construction of piers, wharves, bulkheads, piling, marinas, docks, ramps, floats, mooring buoys, and like structures; (2) the construction of riprap, revetments, groins, breakwaters, and levees; (3) dredging and excavation; and (4) any obstruction or alteration of navigable waters.

Because of the number of applications for the installation and maintenance of boat docks and piers in the Hawaii Kai Marina, the Corps of Engineers has approved the issuance of a general permit, provided that individual property owners meet the limitations, specifications, and conditions laid down by the Corps of Engineers. In almost all other areas of the state, the property owner is required to comply with the standard requirement and obtain a permit for the construction of a dock or pier.

Prior to obtaining a permit from the Corps of Engineers, the property owner must apply for certification from the State of Hawaii Department of Business and Economic Development and the appropriate County Planning Department. Essentially, the certification provides that the proposed activity will comply with and be conducted in a manner consistent with Hawaii's approved Costal Management Program. Other state agencies, such as the Department of Transportation, which has jurisdiction over the waters, and the Department of Land and Natural Resources, which has jurisdiction over submerged lands and the shoreline up to the vegetation line, may also be involved in the certification process. In an attempt by the state government to simplify and expedite the application process for land and water use permits, a program called the Consolidated Application Process (CAP) has been established under the Department of Business and Economic Development. The aim of the CAP program is to assist applicants in obtaining all permits and reviews required for a project in a given location.

IMPORTANT POINT: Whether the proposed improvement is large or small, if your property is a shoreline property or is affected by navigable or United States waters, you can be sure that it will involve several government agencies and that it will take a while before the necessary permits and approvals are issued.

13 What Happens at a Closing?

The contract entered into by a seller and a buyer for the sale and purchase of the seller's property is but the first of many steps leading to the transfer of ownership of the property from the seller to the buyer. Between the time the contract is signed and the actual transfer of ownership, many things must be done so that the transfer can be accomplished smoothly and without a hitch.

What Is a Closing?

In a simplified definition, a *closing* is the process in which the buyer pays for a property and the seller signs and delivers the deed or other conveyance document transferring ownership to the buyer. The date for the closing is agreed upon by the parties in the contract (DROA). On or before the closing date, the parties sign the necessary documents and perform whatever else is necessary to fulfill their end of the bargain at a designated place. In Hawaii, the majority of real estate transactions are closed through an escrow, who is essentially a neutral third party selected by the seller and buyer to conduct the closing. When an escrow is involved, the parties generally sign the documents in the escrow's office, but it is not necessary that the parties sign the documents at the same time or in the presence of the other. Nor is it a legal requirement that the documents be signed at the escrow's office. In those instances when one of the parties resides in a foreign country, the party signs the document at the American embassy or consulate, because conveyance documents require an acknowledgment by a notary public or someone else who is so authorized.

An escrow is an independent, impartial company or person who performs the function of closing a transaction pursuant to an escrow agreement or instructions given by the seller and buyer. The escrow completes the many details that are involved in the transfer of ownership and acts as a coordinator among the many parties to the transaction who include the seller, the buyer, brokers, attorneys, and financial institutions. An escrow provides a central place where all documents can be placed and funds can be deposited until the closing actually takes place. If a transaction is to be closed without the services of an escrow, the parties themselves, their attorneys, or some other person will need to complete the many details involved in closing the real estate transaction. The use of a professional escrow company licensed by the State of Hawaii often proves to be an efficient and reliable way of processing the closing, particularly now that much of the closing work is done by sophisticated computer procedures.

The seller, on the one hand, presents the deed to the escrow with instructions that it be delivered to the buyer only after the buyer has fully performed all the terms and conditions required in the contract. On the other hand, the buyer deposits all of the funds required to be paid to the escrow with instructions that they be paid to the seller upon seller's full performance of his end of the bargain.

EXAMPLE: One of the standard items in the DROA states that the seller "shall deliver to Buyer through escrow a report from a licensed pest control company stating that there is no visible termite infestation in the improvements." If the seller fails to deliver such a report to the escrow, then the seller has not performed all of the terms in the DROA, and escrow will not turn over to the seller the monies paid by the buyer. In the ordinary case, if such a report is not submitted by the seller, the escrow officer, who represents the escrow company, will contact the seller or the seller's broker to remind him of the necessity of furnishing a report to the buyer.

Escrow's Responsibilities Before Closing

After the DROA is signed by the seller and the buyer, the DROA and the buyer's deposit are delivered to the escrow, usually by one of the parties' brokers. The escrow then prepares escrow instructions based on the terms and conditions in the contract, and the buyer's down payment is deposited in the escrow's bank account for safekeeping. In instances where the amount of the deposit is large, the escrow may be instructed to place the funds in an interest-bearing account with the interest to be credited to the buyer. It is credited to the buyer because the money belongs to the buyer until the closing occurs.

Among the instructions given to the escrow is usually the request that a title search report be ordered and that title insurance be obtained. If an existing loan on the property is to be paid off, escrow is instructed to contact the lender to determine the amount necessary to pay off the loan and to prepare a mortgage release that can be recorded as soon as the loan is paid off so that a future title report will not continue to show the seller's mortgage as encumbering the property. On receipt of the title search report, the escrow forwards it to the buyer for review. Escrow will order from a lawyer the deed or other applicable conveyance document transferring ownership to the buyer. Frequently, one of the parties to the contract will specifically name a lawyer to prepare the conveyance document. When no lawyer is named, the escrow will refer the matter to a lawyer of its choice.

Escrow will follow through on all conditions that must be complied with or fulfilled by the parties according to the contract.

Besides the pest control inspection report, escrow will obtain a boundary survey report and a report of the removal of all unacceptable liens and encumbrances on the title. Should there be a tenant occupying the property, it will request the seller to bring in at the time of closing the tenant's security deposit, or it will debit the seller the amount of the security deposit paid by the tenant. If there should be a debit, the amount of the security deposit is deducted from the sales price.

If the buyer is to obtain a loan to purchase the property, the loan documents may be signed by the buyer at the office of the lender, or, as is done frequently, escrow will coordinate the signing of the loan documents with the buyer and the lender so that the promissory note, mortgage, and any other required loan documents are signed and ready to be recorded on the closing date. The funds from the financial institution to pay the purchase price must also be available by the closing date. If the funds are not available, the closing cannot take place, and escrow will have to wait for further instructions from the seller and the buyer.

Prorations

Some expenses and income need to be prorated (computed and divided proportionately) between the seller and the buyer, using the closing as the cutoff date. In Hawaii, prorations include real property taxes, lease rental paid to the lessor—for example, to Bishop Estate—homeowner's insurance premiums if the insurance policy is to be transferred to the buyer, and utilities. Any rent collected by the seller must also be prorated as of the closing date. The escrow will handle the prorations and include them in the closing statement.

> EXAMPLE: When the buyer requests that the seller's homeowner's insurance be transferred to her, she becomes responsible for payment of the policy from the date of the closing until the end of the insurance term. Escrow prorates the insurance premium that has been paid by the seller. If the premium for the insurance is $100 per year and the term starts on January 1 and the closing is

set for July 1, escrow first determines how many months each party is responsible for. In this case, each is responsible for six months, or ½ of the premium (½ of $100 is $50). The seller is liable for $50, and he will be reimbursed the other $50 by the buyer.

Closing Statement

Each party to the transaction receives from the escrow a closing statement, an accounting of the funds payable to the seller and paid by the buyer. The statement is divided into two columns, debits and credits. In the purchaser's statement, the debit column lists all the charges that the purchaser must pay, and the credit column lists all the deposits and mortgages that the purchaser has obtained to pay for the property. The credit column may also include any credit resulting from the prorations. In the seller's statement, the debit column includes all the expenses that the seller is responsible for and any mortgage or other lien payoffs. In the credit column, the seller is credited for the sales price and any prepaid items to be transferred to the buyer.

RESPA

Congress passed the Real Estate Settlement Procedures Act (RESPA), which became effective in 1975. The purpose of the law is to regulate and standardize real estate settlement (closing) practices when federal-related first mortgage loans on residences are made. Such loans include FHA, VA, and other government-backed or federally insured loans. RESPA restricts the amount of advance property tax and insurance payment that a lender can collect from a borrower and place in its reserve account. Under RESPA (1) the buyer receives a Department of Housing and Urban Development (HUD) information booklet from the lender explaining RESPA; (2) he or she receives a good faith estimate of closing costs from the lender; (3) the lender must use the HUD Uniform Settlement Statement; and (4) the borrower has the right to inspect the statement one business day before the closing.

The Typical Closing

No later than the closing day, the seller examines the Seller's Closing Statement and, if the figures are satisfactory, approves it. The deed and the bill of sale (for personal property) will be signed in the presence of a notary public. The seller hands over to the escrow the keys to the property, garage door sensor, security alarm system code numbers, and the lease agreement should there be a tenant occupying the property.

The buyer reviews and approves the Buyer's Closing Statement. She signs any loan documents that have not been signed and brings in any additional funds necessary to pay for the property and closing costs. Prior to the closing the buyer or her attorney will have reviewed all conveyance documents transferring ownership to her, the updated title search report, and the title insurance policy.

It is customary in Hawaii for the real estate agent to be present at the closing to assist his client and to answer any question that the client may have regarding the transaction or the closing.

The escrow presents each party with his or her closing statement to be approved by the party. The approval of the statement constitutes a final settlement between the seller and the buyer.

If the property is leasehold, the assignment of lease assigning the lease from the seller to the buyer must be consented to by the lessor. The escrow will obtain that consent as soon as the assignment of lease is signed by both parties. Without the consent, the assignment of lease will not be recorded and this in turn will delay the closing. Therefore, the signing of the assignment of the lease by the seller and buyer and the signing of the consent of the lessor are all done prior to the closing date.

It is the customary practice in Hawaii for the conveyance and loan documents to be recorded on the business day following the signing of the documents. Only after the recording is confirmed are all funds disbursed to the seller, the real estate agents, and the seller's lender. Then, within a week or two, the buyer will receive a copy of the recorded deed and the mortgage document, the seller will receive a copy of the release of mortgage, and the lender will receive its mortgage document.

IMPORTANT POINT: There are many important documents, legal papers, and forms that need to be prepared and ready for signatures by the date of closing. A number of details must be complied with and satisfied by the closing. Accurate calculations must be made. For a smooth and successful closing, it is almost mandatory to hire an escrow company. Nothing is more aggravating than to see the successful negotiation for the sale and purchase of real estate botched up by someone inexperienced or unfamiliar with closing requirements.

14 In What Tenancy Should the Property Be Held?

In the purchase of real estate, the buyer receives a *conveyance document* from the seller in which the seller transfers all right, title, and interest in the property to the buyer to evidence the transfer of ownership. When the real estate involved is fee simple property, the customary conveyance document is a deed. When leasehold property is sold, the conveyance document is an assignment of lease. Currently, a *condominium conveyance document* transferring both the apartment unit and the interest in the land is generally used when a condominium is transferred. The land on which the condominium building is situated may be a leasehold property, and the condominium apartment itself may be owned in fee simple.

In real estate, frequent reference is made to *title*. Title means the right to property or ownership of property. The *title holder* is the owner of the property.

EXAMPLE: The names shown on a deed are Jim Jones and Cindi Jones. The question is asked, "Who is on title?" This is a way of asking who the owners are. The answer is, "The title holders are Jim Jones and Cindi Jones."

The conveyance document also indicates the *tenancy* in which title to a property is held. There are different tenancies, or ways of holding ownership of real estate. In fact, one of the questions that a buyer must answer on a contract to purchase property is, in what tenancy is the title to be held?

It is important that the tenancy you select is the appropriate one for you, because the tenancy will affect your right to sell or transfer the real estate, your right to choose the owner of your property upon your death, and the right of any of your creditors in the property. The tenancy may also have implications with regard to federal estate and gift tax.

Real estate can be owned by a single individual or by multiple parties. Tenancy is particularly critical in instances in which real estate is owned by two or more owners, because the ownership is concurrent rather than successive.

EXAMPLE: Jim Jones and Cindi Jones are title holders of the same property. They own the property concurrently, that is, they have the same rights at the same time. It is not a situation where Jim Jones first owns the real estate in his own right and at a subsequent time Cindi Jones becomes owner. Both of them own the property together at the same time.

The types of tenancy are *tenancy in severalty, tenancy by the entirety, joint tenancy,* and *tenancy in common.* Tenancy by the entirety, joint tenancy, and tenancy in common are forms of multiple ownership. In other words, more than one person holds title to the property.

Tenancy in Severalty

When title is held by one person, whether that person is single or married, ownership is deemed to be a tenancy in severalty. It is a sole ownership of the property. This form of ownership provides flexibility to the owner, because there are no co-owners involved in making decisions. You as owner alone control how the property is to be used. If the property is rented, you decide how much rent to charge and how the property is to be managed. When you decide to sell the property, you alone determine when to sell, the sale price, and the terms and conditions of the sale. As the sole owner of the property, you own the property outright in your name until your death. You determine who the owners of the property shall be after your death by naming beneficiaries in your will or trust. You have absolute control over the property.

One drawback in the sole ownership of a property is the necessity of transferring title by a court proceeding upon the owner's death. The legal requirement of transferring title to the property by a court proceeding is commonly known as a *probate* proceeding. This proceeding takes time and money. The personal representative (the executor or the administrator) who handles all probate matters on behalf of the deceased owner, and the attorney handling the probate must be paid fees based on a percentage of the value of the assets. Also, probate matters are public, and all information filed in court is open to public scrutiny.

Another drawback is the ability of a creditor to *execute* solely owned property. If a creditor obtained a judgment against you, such a person, known as a *judgment creditor,* would have the legal right to execute the property to satisfy the judgment by selling it.

Tenancy by the Entirety

Tenancy by the entirety is a form of tenancy specifically intended for a married couple. The two key characteristics are a right of survivorship, by which the surviving spouse becomes the sole owner of the entire real estate on the death of the first spouse, and the stipulation that neither spouse can dispose of his or her interest in the property during the lifetime of the other without the agreement of the other spouse.

EXAMPLE: Henry Hale and Harriet Hale, husband and wife, acquire a house and lot in Paia, Maui. The deed to them reads: "Henry Hale and Harriet Hale, as Tenants by the Entirety, with the right of survivorship." Upon the death of Henry Hale, Harriet Hale automatically becomes sole owner of the house and lot.

It is not necessary to draw up any document showing Harriet Hale to be the sole owner of the property after the death of her husband, nor is it necessary to probate Henry Hale's will to transfer his right, title, and interest in the property to Harriet Hale. The surviving spouse becomes the exclusive owner of the property by operation of law upon the death of the first spouse.

If, for any reason, both spouses decide to convert the tenancy by the entirety to another form of tenancy, they must both sign the appropriate conveyance document expressly indicating their intention to convert the tenancy. In other words, one of the spouses cannot convert the tenancy without joint action of the other. However, in the case of a divorce, the tenancy automatically changes to a tenancy in common for the reason that a tenancy by the entirety exists only when the co-owners are husband and wife.

An important feature of the tenancy by the entirety in Hawaii is that the interest of a husband or a wife in the real estate is not subject to the claims of his or her individual creditors during the joint lives of the spouses. In a landmark Hawaii case, the Supreme Court stated:

> Neither husband nor wife has a separate divisible interest in the property held by the entirety that can be conveyed or reached by execution. . . .
>
> A joint tenancy may be destroyed by voluntary execution, or by compulsory partition, but a tenancy by the entirety may not. The indivisibility of the estate, except by the joint action of the spouses, is an indispensable feature of the tenancy by the entirety.[13]

Therefore, as long as both husband and wife are living, no creditor of either the husband or the wife can seize the property to satisfy a judgment obtained against one of the spouses. Of course, if a judgment is obtained against both spouses, the property may be executed by the judgment creditor. If a judgment had been obtained against one spouse and then the other spouse was to die, the property could be executed, because the surviving spouse would then be the sole owner of the property.

Note that you cannot devise (grant) by will a property held in tenancy by the entirety unless you are the surviving spouse. The property automatically becomes the sole property of the surviving spouse upon the death of the first spouse.

Joint Tenancy

Another form of multiple-party ownership distinguished by the right of survivorship is joint tenancy. However, in a joint tenancy, the owners are not husband and wife.

In creating a joint tenancy, four unities must be present: (1) time, (2) title, (3) interest, and (4) possession.

Unity of time means that all of the joint tenants must acquire the interest in the property at the same time.

> EXAMPLE: Gabriel Goodheart conveys his property to his sons, Tom and Dick, as joint tenants with right of survivorship. Each has received his interest in the property at the same time. A new owner may not join the original joint tenancy, because the unity of time would be lacking. Therefore, if a third son, Harry, acquires an interest in the property at a later date, the joint tenancy no longer exists.

Unity of title means that the owners must acquire their interest in the property from the same source, such as the same deed or will. In the above example, Tom and Dick received their interest through Gabriel Goodheart's deed, which fulfills the unity of title requirement.

Unity of interest means that the joint tenants own an identical interest in the property, and each owner has exactly the same right in the property. In other words, each joint tenant holds equal ownership interest in the property.

Unity of possession means that all of the owners enjoy the same undivided possession of the whole property. Each of them has the right to use the entire property and not simply a portion of the property.

> EXAMPLE: Tom and Dick both own twenty acres of farmland. Each of them is entitled to use and enjoy the entire twenty acres of the land and not just a portion of the farm.

With regard to the right of survivorship, the last surviving joint tenant becomes the sole owner of the property.

EXAMPLE: The Fantastic Four is a group of four joint tenants. Upon the death of one, the remaining three own the property. Upon the death of the next joint tenant, the remaining two own the property. Finally, upon the death of the second-to-last owner, the last remaining joint tenant becomes the sole owner of the entire real estate.

Because of the right of survivorship feature, a joint tenant may not devise his or her interest in the property by will. Only the last survivor has an interest in the property to transfer.

A joint tenancy can be terminated by destroying any of the four unities. For example, one joint tenant can convey his or her interest in the property to an outsider. In the case of a dispute among the joint tenants, the owners may file a *partition suit* to dissolve the co-ownership of the property. Should the court determine that the land cannot be divided into equal parts, it may order the land to be sold and the proceeds to be divided equally among the joint tenants.

Tenancy in Common

When two or more persons own a single property as tenants in common, each is deemed to own an undivided interest in the whole property, which means that each owner has a right to possession of the entire property. However, the interest of each owner need not necessarily be the same. Moreover, in a tenancy in common, each owner can sell, mortgage, transfer, or devise his interest without the consent of the other co-owners, because each owner has a separate legal title to his undivided interest. In effect, each owner holds that interest as though he were a sole owner.

EXAMPLE: A grantor conveys a parcel of land to Urban Uno, Darcy Dos, and Theodore Tres as tenants in common. Because there is no indication of the proportion of each owner's interest, it is deemed to be equal. As a tenant in common, Urban Uno is permitted to sell his interest to a third party, and Darcy Dos can mortgage her undivided interest to secure a loan, and, finally, Theodore Tres may devise his interest in the property by will to his wife.

As a tenant in common owning an undivided interest in the entire parcel, Urban Uno cannot take and use a specific one-third section of the land and exclude Darcy and Theodore from that portion of the property, because each of them owns an interest in the entire parcel of land.

In Hawaii, if there is no indication of how a property is to be held among co-owners, the law specifically provides that each of them shall hold the property as a tenant in common.

Each co-owner is responsible for payment of a share of the taxes, upkeep, utilities, maintenance, and other costs and expenses. Any income earned from the property must be divided according to proportionate interest in the property.

There is no right of survivorship in a tenancy in common. Consequently, an owner's interest passes on to the heirs or to the beneficiaries named in the owner's will. The owner's interest is subject to claim by creditors.

In case of a dispute, a partition suit may be filed to divide the property into distinct physical portions. If it is not possible to divide the property, it will be sold and the proceeds divided according to each owner's proportionate share.

A husband and wife may own real estate as tenants in common. This option is occasionally selected for estate planning purposes, that is, owners of real estate have documents drawn up to transfer real estate in anticipation of their eventual demise.

IMPORTANT POINT: You can acquire real estate individually or with others, and each way has its advantages and disadvantages. When real estate is acquired by multiple parties, the tenancy of the parties is important, because certain consequences flow from the tenancy, particularly with respect to the ownership and transfer of the property. In selecting the tenancy, therefore, more than casual thought should be given. The tenancy best suited for particular persons must be determined on a case-by-case basis, paying particular attention to the needs and desires of the owners.

15 Should You Obtain Title Insurance?

```
COMMITMENT FOR TITLE INSURANCE

INFORMATION

    The Title Insurance Commitment is a legal contract between you and the company. It is issued to
show the basis on which we will issue a Title Insurance Policy to you. The Policy will insure you against
certain risks to the land title, subject to the limitations shown in the Policy.

    The Company will give you a sample of the Policy form, if you ask.

    The Commitment is based on the land title as of the Commitment Date. Any changes in the land
title or the transaction may affect the Commitment and the Policy.

    The Commitment is subject to its Requirements, Exceptions and Conditions.

    THIS INFORMATION IS NOT PART OF THE TITLE INSURANCE COMMITMENT.


                                TABLE OF CONTENTS

                                                            Page
AGREEMENT TO ISSUE POLICY                                    1

SCHEDULE A
```

Before the closing of a transaction in which you are buying real estate, you may be asked whether you wish to obtain title insurance. Title insurance insures a property owner against loss arising from title defects.

Title, as you recall, is the evidence of ownership of real estate, and proof of good title is contained in the title search report presented to you at or before closing. No matter how careful the person preparing a title report may be, there is no guarantee that the report is one hundred percent accurate. The title searcher may not be negligent, but the information upon which the report is based may still be false or inaccurate.

EXAMPLE: The chain of title indicates that a property had been conveyed to the seller, Ned Nogood, by Ira Innocento. Relying on the title report, a buyer purchases the property from Ned Nogood. After the buyer acquires the property, Ira Innocento demands that the buyer get off his property. The buyer learns that

107

Ira Innocento had never signed any deed to Ned Nogood but that Ned Nogood had fraudulently conveyed the property to himself by forging Ira Innocento's signature on the deed. The person preparing the title report was correct in showing a deed from Ira Innocento to Ned Nogood, but she could not have known of the forgery by Ned Nogood. The forgery is a defect in the title that would be covered by title insurance. The buyer has suffered a loss, because the property that he purchased in good faith from Ned Nogood is rightfully owned by Ira Innocento.

Other instances of title defect include negligence by the abstractor, a mistake in the boundary description, the failure to mention an easement or encumbrance affecting the property, and execution of a conveyance instrument by a minor or incompetent person.

When a title company in Hawaii is requested to issue title insurance to a buyer, the title company first examines all of the public records relating to the property. The examination or search is done by an abstractor or a title searcher, and the information that is gathered becomes the title search report. The title insurance is contingent on the information contained in the title search report. If a defect is mentioned in the report, the title insurance company may insure the title "around the defect," that is, the defect is specifically excluded. The title company may charge separately for the title search report and the title insurance.

The amount of the insurance coverage is generally equal to the amount of the purchase price, and there is a one-time charge for the insurance, consisting of a single premium payment. The insurance remains effective as long as the buyer or the buyer's heirs have an interest in the property. Therefore, each time the property is sold, a new policy must be purchased by the new owner.

Title insurance has caused lenders to be more willing to make loans to real property owners. It has made mortgage borrowing easier and less expensive for property owners, because the financial institutions are protected against the risk of loss stemming from a defect in title. Theoretically, as a result of such protection, interest on loans is lower as well.

IMPORTANT POINT: The chance of a defect in title may be minuscule in Hawaii. However, the importance of having title insurance, like all other insurance, is not evident until trouble strikes. It is wiser to obtain title insurance when real estate is purchased than to risk purchasing the property without the insurance. If a defect is found, the cost, time, and effort is likely to be far more expensive than the insurance.

16 What Is Recordation?

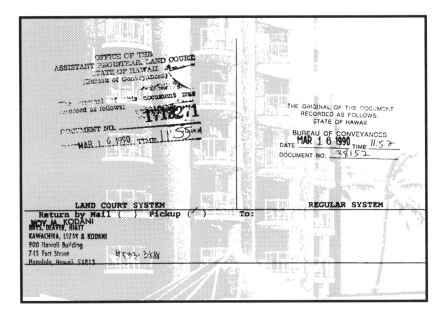

In Hawaii, as in other states, the statute provides for the recording of real estate documents. The purpose of recording a document is to provide notice to all the world of the estate, right, title, or interest that has been created, transferred, or encumbered by the document. Subsequently, everyone is deemed to know about the document. In Hawaii, there is only one recording office, the Bureau of Conveyances, located in Honolulu. The Bureau of Conveyances is administered by the State of Hawaii Department of Accounting and General Services. Unlike other jurisdictions in which documents are recorded in the county in which the real estate is located, in Hawaii documents involving real estate located in the counties of Kauai, Maui, and Hawaii, as well as the City and County of Honolulu are all recorded in the Bureau of Conveyances. The records are open to the general public.

The recording of a document is handled in the majority of cases by the escrow company that handles the closing of the transaction. In other instances, the attorney who prepares the document, the real estate broker representing the buyer, the financial institution making a loan to the property owner, or even the property owner may record the document. It is important for the owner of property to record all real estate documents. If both an innocent third party and a property owner both suffer damages due to the failure of the owner to record the document, the owner may not recover his loss but the innocent third party may do so. In reaching such a decision, the courts will weigh the equities of both the owner and the innocent third party. In other words, they will take into account the fact that the owner could have prevented his loss by recording the document and hold that the innocent third party should not be made to suffer for the owner's negligence.

The recording statute in Hawaii requires that all documents be *acknowledged* before being recorded. An acknowledgment is a formal declaration by the person signing the document that he or she did in fact sign the document. An acknowledgment is usually taken by a notary public or other public official authorized by law to take acknowledgments. The purpose of the acknowledgment is to ascertain that the person who signs the document is the same person named in the document, that the person signing the document knew what he or she was signing, and that the signing was a free and voluntary act of the person. Acknowledgments are taken to ensure that the public records are free of the possibility of forgery and fraud.

For recordation purposes in Hawaii, there are two different types of real property, both processed at the Bureau of Conveyances. One is referred to as regular system property and the other as Land Court system property. The value of a property is not affected by its being either regular system or Land Court system.

Regular System

For regular system property, the real estate document to be recorded is photocopied by the Bureau of Conveyances and returned to the owner. The photocopied document is arranged in the chronological order of its presentation to the Bureau of Conveyances for recordation and bound with other documents into a book, formerly referred to as *liber* (Latin for book). In the past, the recordation information consisted of book and page number in which the document was recorded. The current practice is to assign a document number to each recorded document.

In order to facilitate the research of public records, the Bureau of Conveyances has established a system of indexes similar to the systems used in other states. There is an index of grantors (persons transferring) and one of grantees (persons receiving). Each index, arranged in alphabetical order for a specific year, is bound in a separate book. The grantor index, for example, lists all the grantors named in documents recorded for the particular year along with the name of the grantee and the book and page number where the photocopied document can be found. Since 1989, the document number is shown in place of book and page number. Without the grantor and grantee indexes, a person researching the public records would need to inspect every document in every book to track down a particular document. The grantor and grantee indexes save time and effort for the researcher.

For all intents and purposes, the Bureau of Conveyances accepts any type of document for recordation in the Regular System as long as it conforms to required recordation format. The Land Court system, however, has in the past required a certificate of title or a transfer certificate of title to be filed along with the document being recorded.

> EXAMPLE: You, as a real estate owner, intend to file (record) a deed at the Land Court section of the Bureau of Conveyances. Formerly, you also had to file either the certificate of title or the transfer certificate of title that was issued to you as the owner of that particular real estate. Because the Land Court now retains all certificates of title and transfer certificates of title, this is no longer a requirement.

Land Court System

The main difference between Land Court property and regular system property is that the title of Land Court property is registered—just as title to an automobile is registered—whereas title to regular system property is not. Another significant difference is that there can be no adverse possession of Land Court property. A continuous, open, notorious, hostile, and exclusive possession of another person's regular system land for twenty years may ripen into a claim for ownership by the squatter or user. The distinction between regular system property and Land Court property is also important from the standpoint of legal requirements involved in recording a document. The Land Court system has more requirements than the regular system and is more complicated.

The Hawaii Land Court system is based on the Torrens system, named after Sir Robert Richard Torrens, who established the Torrens land title registration system in South Australia in 1858. The Hawaii legislature enacted the Torrens system into law in 1903 to "create a system of dealing with land which is simple, rapid, inexpensive and secure." It set up a system of registering land title with the Land Court and conveying such land by means of certificates of title.

Two basic principles underlie the land title registration system: accuracy and indefeasibility of title, that is, title cannot be defeated or revoked.

When a land owner files the application to register title, the parcel of land must be accurately described in the application and on the map showing the location of the land. The map will be referred by the Land Court to the state surveyor, who will verify the accuracy of the information contained on the map and submit a report of his or her findings to the Land Court. Also, the applicant's title to the land must be definitely and clearly proven through a required judicial proceeding. After the hearing, if the Land Court finds that the applicant at the time of filing the application or subsequently had title to the land and that the title is proper for registration, a decree of confirmation and registration is entered. The title registration will include any valid liens or encumbrances existing at the time of registration. The effect of the registration removes any cloud on the title of the registered land. The registration acts to "quiet" the title. In other words, it lays to rest any question or dispute there may have been on the title to the land. The decree is final and conclusive against all persons.

Title to Land Court property is deemed to be indefeasible. In other words, a person is not required to look beyond the register book to determine the validity of the title to the land. If any flaws have not been eliminated or stated in the certificate of title, the doctrine of indefeasibility will cure such defects. The registration system was adopted to save a person the trouble and the expense of having to determine the validity of title to land.

Every decree of registration binds the land. In effect, once land is registered, it remains registered and no further registration or renewal is required. Consequently, even if the original applicant conveys the land to another person, the subsequent owners need not file a new application to register the land.

In the past, the Land Court issued a *certificate of title* to the original applicant. Thereafter, if the registered land was conveyed to another person, the original applicant submitted the certificate of title together with the deed or other conveyance instrument to the Land Court counter at the Bureau of Conveyances at the time of filing the conveyance document, and a new certificate was issued to the new owner called a *transfer certificate of title*. However, under the present system, the transfer certificate of title (TCT) now remains at the Bureau of Conveyances.

The Bureau of Conveyances notes the names of any new owners of the property after the transfer or sale of the property. Any other important matters that may affect the land or the owner, such as, a mortgage, long-term lease, marriage, or death of the owner, are noted on the certificate.

Whenever any document or conveyance instrument involving Land Court property is filed with the Land Court, a document number is assigned to it. The description of the document and the document number are noted on the original certificate of title or the TCT, which are retained in the Land Court section of the Bureau of Conveyances. Because all documents are noted on the certificate of title or the TCT, a person researching a particular Land Court property is able to determine the current status of the property by reading the certificate of title or the TCT.

IMPORTANT POINT: There have not been many applications to register title with the Land Court. The lack of applicants can be attributed in part to the high cost of obtaining an abstract of title for a particular parcel of land. Moreover, there is no longer a real need to register title, because the modern practice is to purchase title insurance to cover any title problem that may arise. Protection against adverse possession of a property is no longer as critical with the increase in urbanization of real estate and the value of property throughout the state. Most owners are careful to protect their property and be sure no stranger is using it without permission.

REFERENCE: Land Court Registration. Chapter 501, *Hawaii Revised Statutes*.

17 What Is Conveyance Tax?

HAWAII
FORM P-64A
(Rev. 1979)
SEE INSTRUCTIONS ON REVERSE SIDE

STATE OF HAWAII
DEPARTMENT OF TAXATION
Conveyance Tax Certificate

TAX KEY

Z	S	PLAT	PARCEL	HPR NO
1	3	045	063	95

Island _OAHU_ Apt. No. _987_

In compliance with Chapter 247 HRS, as amended, I (we) do hereby certify that to the best of my (our) knowledge and belief the actual and full consideration paid on the conveyance to which this certificate is appended is: (fill in A or B)

A. Deed, Agreement of Sale, Assignment of Lease, or like Document

Sale Price $200,000

Special Assessment

Other Consideration

Deduct: Personal Property 10,000

Actual & Full Consideration $190,000

B. Lease, Sublease, Extension, or Amendment of Lease
please provide rentals and terms here
if lease is unrecorded or does not recite rentals

Term: _____ years Begin: _____
Rent:
1st period _____ yrs @ $ _____ /yr.
2nd period _____ yrs @ $ _____ /yr.
3rd period _____ yrs @ $ _____ /yr.
4th period _____ yrs @ $ _____ /yr.

Rent Capitalized at 6% = $ _____
Plus Price Paid for Leasehold Land and any Buildings + $ _____
Deduct Personal Property $ _____
Actual and Full Consideration $ _____

August 9, 1990
Date of Transaction

The "Date of Transaction" is the date the document is executed, or the date of the last acknowledgment. The Conveyance Tax Certificate must be filed within 90 days after the date of the transaction. Penalty of 5% per month up to an aggregate of 25% shall be imposed for late filing. I (We) further certify and understand that the penalty for false declaration is a fine of not

Hawaii statute requires the payment of a conveyance tax on all transfers or conveyance of realty or any interest in realty, whether by deed, lease or sublease whose term is five years or more, assignment of lease, agreement of sale, assignment of agreement of sale, or any other document whereby land, interest in land, or other realty is sold. The tax is based on the actual and full consideration paid or to be paid for the realty. The current rate is $.05 per $100 of the consideration paid for the realty.

EXAMPLE: Algin Affluent purchases a Waikiki condominium penthouse for $900,000. The conveyance tax is $450, computed as follows:

$$\$900,000 \div \$100 = \$9,000$$
$$\$9,000 \times \$0.05 = \$450.00$$

The grantor, lessor, sublessor, assignor, transferror, seller, or any other person conveying the real estate is liable for payment of the tax. If the party conveying the real estate is the federal, state, or municipal government, then the tax is paid by the party to whom the real estate is conveyed. The law requires that the tax be paid no later than ninety days after the transaction. This tax is a one-time tax.

The conveyance tax is customarily paid when the conveyance document is presented to the Bureau of Conveyances for recordation. The law requires that it be paid prior to the recordation. As evidence of the tax payment, seals are imprinted on the document indicating the amount of the tax paid. As indicated in the discussion of real estate appraisals in chapter 5, you can determine the price of the real estate from the total conveyance tax paid.

A certificate of conveyance must be appended to the conveyance document that is to be recorded, setting forth the actual and full consideration of the property. The certificate is transmitted to the Director of Finance of the county in which the property is located by the Bureau of Conveyances. By means of the certificate of conveyances, the Director of Finance keeps track of all the real estate transactions occurring in the county.

Exemptions to the tax include the following: (1) any document or instrument given to secure a debt or obligation, such as a mortgage, (2) any document or instrument confirming or correcting a previously recorded document, (3) any document or instrument between a husband and wife or parent and child in which there is only a nominal amount paid, such as "$1.00 and love," (4) any document or instrument in which the amount paid is $100 or less, and (5) any document or instrument conveying real property pursuant to an agreement of sale or assignment of an agreement of sale. Effective November 13, 1989, all exemptions to the conveyance tax must be approved by the Department of Taxation. The document or instrument together with an affidavit for an exemption from the conveyance tax must be submitted to the Department of Taxation before recordation.

IMPORTANT POINT: The present rate of the conveyance tax is not high. However, it is a cost that must be considered by the seller of a property, because the cost is deducted from the sales price of the real estate. Proposals have been made to adjust or increase the conveyance tax as a way of discouraging the escalation of real property prices.

REFERENCE: Conveyance Tax. Chapter 247, *Hawaii Revised Statutes*.

18 What Should You Know About Real Property Tax?

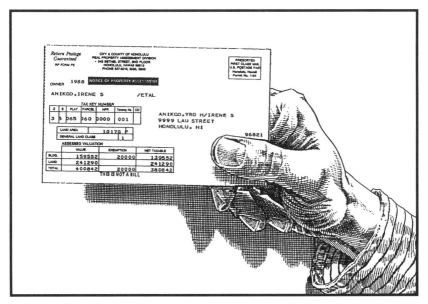

One of the most common ways of raising revenue in Hawaii is the imposition and collection of real property tax. All functions, powers, and duties relating to the taxation of real property have, since July 1, 1981, been exercised exclusively by the counties and not by the state as had formerly been the case. The county ordinances relating to the real property tax are essentially similar. Because almost 80 percent of the population of the state resides in the City and County of Honolulu, the information in this chapter will focus on Honolulu.

Tax Base and Rate

Except for certain exemptions, all real property in the state is subject to a tax on 100 percent of its fair market value. The *tax base* is therefore 100 percent.

The council of each county determines the *tax rate* for imposing

119

tax on real property for each tax year. The tax rate must be adopted on or before June 20 preceding the tax year. For real property tax purposes, the *tax year* means the fiscal year beginning July 1 and ending June 30 of the following calendar year.

Whatever the tax base or rate may be, each taxable parcel of real property is subject to a minimum tax of $7.00 per year.

Valuation of Real Property

The director of finance is responsible for determining the fair market value of all taxable real property and assessing the value annually by "the market data and cost approaches to value using appropriate systematic methods suitable for mass valuation of properties for taxation purposes." *Assessment* means setting a value for taxation purposes.

> EXAMPLE: If the director of finance from the available information and data determines that the fair value of the land at 43-210 Kam Highway, Haleiwa, is $220,000, the official value for real property tax purposes, or the *assessed value,* will be $220,000.

The director is required to value and assess the improvements and buildings separately from the land. The valuation must be pursuant to an appropriate systematic method and must be applied uniformly and equally throughout the state. The method of valuation must be kept by the director so taxpayers know what method is used to value real property in the county in case there is any question on the assessed value of a property.

The valuation depends on the classification of the land, which takes into consideration its highest and best use. The general classes of property are (1) improved residential, (2) unimproved residential, (3) apartment, (4) hotel and resort, (5) commercial, (6) industrial, (7) agricultural, and (8) conservation. In assigning the land to one of the classifications, the director is required to give major consideration to the districting established by the State Land Use Commission, the districting established by the county in its general plan and zoning ordinance, use classifications established in the general plan of the state, and other factors influencing the highest and best use of the land.

Exemptions

A claim for exemption must be filed with the Department of Finance on or before December 31 preceding the tax year for which such exemption is claimed. Thus, in order for the claim for exemption to have been granted for tax year commencing July 1, 1990, the claim must have been filed on or before December 31, 1989. Once an exemption is allowed, it will have continuing effect until it is disallowed, voided, or expires under certain conditions. Some of the important exemptions follow.

Homes. Property owned and occupied as an individual's principal home as of the date of assessment receives an exemption of $40,000. A taxpayer between the ages of 55 and 59 is entitled to a multiple exemption of 1.5 times, or $60,000; a taxpayer between the ages of 60 and 64 is entitled to a multiple exemption of 2.0 or $80,000; a taxpayer between the ages of 64 and 69 is entitled to a multiple exemption of 2.5, or $100,000; a taxpayer 70 years old or over is entitled to a multiple exemption of 3.0, or $120,000. The exemption is first deducted from the value of the residential structure and then from the land. A husband and wife owning property jointly are entitled to a multiple exemption when at least one spouse qualifies each year for the applicable multiple exemption. A "home" includes any residence on land held by a lessee under a lease for a term of five years or more that has been duly recorded and in which lease the lessee agrees to pay all real property taxes during the term of the lease.

Disabled veteran. Real property owned and occupied as a home by any person totally disabled owing to injuries received while on duty with the U.S. armed forces (or by a widow or widower of such a person) is totally exempt.

Disability. Any person who is blind, deaf, or totally disabled is entitled to an exemption of up to but not exceeding $25,000.

Other exemptions are given to persons afflicted with leprosy, nonprofit medical indemnity or hospital service associations, charitable organizations, property in urban districts dedicated by the owner for landscaping, open spaces, and public recreation, air pollution control facilities, and alternate energy improvements.

Notice of Assessment and the Appeal Process

On or before March 15 preceding the tax year, the director must notify each property owner of the assessment for the tax year, setting forth separately the valuation of the buildings and the land, the exemption, if any, the net taxable value of the buildings, and the net taxable value of all other real property exclusive of the buildings.

Any taxpayer who deems himself aggrieved (to have suffered a loss) by an assessment made by the director or by the director's refusal to allow any exemption may appeal the assessment to a board of review or the state tax appeal court on or before April 9 preceding the tax year.

Tax Payments

The real property tax year begins on July 1 and the tax is payable in two equal installments. The annual billing date is July 20, the first payment is due August 20, and the second payment is due February 20. Any unpaid tax becomes delinquent. The statute imposes a penalty up to 10 percent of the delinquent tax. In addition, interest at the rate of ⅔ of 1 percent per month is imposed on any delinquent tax and penalty until paid.

Tax Lien

Every tax due on a real property is a lien upon the property that attaches as of July 1 of the tax year. The lien continues for six years if the tax remains unpaid. Real property with a lien for unpaid tax may be sold by the director without a lawsuit. If a lien exists for three years, the real property can be sold at public auction to the highest bidder for cash to satisfy the lien. The sale must be conducted at a public place after notice has been published at least once a week for at least four successive weeks in any newspaper of general circulation. Written notice of the sale must be given to the property owner at least forty-five days prior to the date of the sale.

After the sale, the director prepares and delivers the appropriate conveyance instrument vesting title in the property to the purchaser. The deed to the property must be recorded within sixty days after the sale. However, any taxpayer may *redeem* the property sold to satisfy a tax lien within one year from the date of the sale, or, if the deed from the director to the purchaser was not recorded within sixty days, the taxpayer may redeem the property within one year from the date of the recordation of the deed. In such a case, the taxpayer regains possession of the property by payment of the delinquent taxes, penalty, interest, and costs.

> EXAMPLE: Harry Hardluck fails to pay his real property taxes for four years, and the property is sold by the director at a public auction to Ovid Opportunist. Eleven months later, Harry Hardluck is able to reacquire his property by paying Ovid Opportunist the same amount paid by Ovid to the director plus interest on the total amount at the rate of 12 percent per annum, and costs of the auction.

Tax Map Key

The director of taxation of the State of Hawaii is required by law to provide for each taxation district maps showing all parcels, blocks, lots, or other divisions of land based on ownership and their areas or dimensions that are numbered or otherwise designated in a systematic manner for convenience of identification, valuation, and assessment. The maps must show the names of owners of each division of land and must be revised from time to time as ownerships change and further divisions of parcels occur. For taxation purposes, the state is divided into four taxation districts: first district—City and County of Honolulu; second district—County of Maui; third district—County of Hawaii; fourth district—County of Kauai. Each division of land is identified by a tax map key number. A prospective buyer of a parcel of land wishing to find out the owners of the surrounding properties or other information, such as easements affecting the property to be purchased, can learn such information from examining the tax map by first determining the county in which the property is located and then proceeding to the map showing the property in question.

EXAMPLE: Tax Map Key 6-8-03:500
The first number, 6, refers to the zone. The second number, 8, refers to the section. The third number, 3, refers to the plat, and the fourth number is the number of the parcel. The prospective buyer would track down the map showing zone 6, section 8, plat 3. Parcel 500 would be shown on that particular map.

IMPORTANT POINT: Because the real property tax is the prime source of revenue for the counties, the ordinances are amended whenever the financial conditions call for more revenue. Therefore, it is best to verify the current real property tax laws by contacting the office of the director of finance of the county in which a real property is located.

REFERENCE: Real Property Tax. Chapter 8, *Revised Ordinances of Honolulu, 1978.*

19 What Are Your Rights When the Other Party Breaks the Contract?

STATE OF HAWAII CIRCUIT COURT OF THE FIRST CIRCUIT	SUMMONS TO ANSWER CIVIL COMPLAINT	
PLAINTIFF JON HOMESEEKER AND ANN HOMESEEKER	vs	DEFENDANT BART BADPERSON
PLAINTIFF'S ATTORNEY (NAME, ADDRESS, TEL. NO.) Roy M. Kodani 691-0 Suite 900, Hawaii Tower 745 Fort Street Honolulu, Hawaii 96813 833-3888		

TO THE DEFENDANT(S):

You are hereby summoned and required to serve upon plaintiff's attorney, whose address complaint which is attached. This action must be taken within twenty days after service of this the day of service.

If you fail to make your answer within the twenty day time limit, judgment by default will b demanded in the complaint.

Real estate purchases are not always successfully consummated. For one reason or another, the seller may refuse to sell or the buyer may not go through with the purchase of the property. What are your rights, as the innocent party to such a contract, when the other party fails to perform as agreed to in the contract? What are the remedies available to you in the case of default? The Deposit Receipt, Offer, and Acceptance (DROA) agreement expressly provides certain remedies, which are essentially the usual legal remedies available to the nondefaulting party.

If the buyer fails to pay the full purchase price or complete the purchase as agreed in the DROA, the seller may do one of the following: (1) The seller may bring an action for damages for breach of contract. The general rule is that the party to a contract who is damaged by the breach is entitled to compensation for the breach insofar as compensation can be made by money. Compensation is intended to put the party in the same financial position he or she would have occupied if the contract had been performed. The mea-

125

sure of damages is the actual loss sustained by reason of the breach, usually the value of the contract including any profits that could have been earned and expenses incurred in reliance on the performance of the contract.

EXAMPLE: If the purchase price of a property is $100,000 and the closing costs are $1,000, the seller is entitled to sue for $101,000.

(2) The seller may retain the initial deposit and all additional deposits paid by the buyer as *liquidated damages*. Liquidated damages refers to the amount that the seller and the buyer agreed to pay in case either of them breaks the contract. The amount of damages is decided in advance and stated in the contract.

EXAMPLE: The buyer pays $5,000 as initial deposit and another $5,000 as additional deposit upon seller's acceptance of the buyer's offer. Both seller and buyer agree that the liquidated damages in the event of a default by the buyer will be the initial and additional deposits. Seller may retain the total of $10,000 as liquidated damages.

(3) The seller may hold the buyer responsible for any cost incurred relative to the contract.

EXAMPLE: Usually, the seller is obligated to deliver a title search report of the property to be sold. In case of a breach by the buyer, the buyer is responsible for payment for such report, which is a cost incurred by the seller.

If the seller fails to perform the seller's obligations under the contract and the buyer is not in default, the buyer may seek one of the following remedies: (1) The buyer may bring an action against the seller for damages for breach of contract. In Hawaii, the courts have adopted the American rule[13] of measuring damages for the buyer when the seller defaults.[14] Under the American rule, the buyer is entitled to recover ordinary contract damages, measured by the difference between the contract price and the market value of the land, together with any partial payments of the price. The market value is determined at the time of the breach. The buyer is also entitled to recover attorney's fees in those instances where the statute, contract, or other document provides for attorney's fees.

> EXAMPLE: If the contract price for a property is $300,000 and the market value of the property is $350,000 at the time of the breach, the buyer's damage is $50,000 plus any deposit paid by the buyer.

(2) The buyer may file and maintain an action for *specific performance* of the contract. An action for specific performance seeks to compel the seller to deliver title to the real property. The rationale for this action is that no parcel of land has a counterpart anywhere else, and duplication is impossible by the expenditure of any amount of money. In other words, no two properties are exactly alike. Each is unique. Rather than seeking compensation, you seek specific performance, since money damages would be inadequate, impractical or doubtful.

> EXAMPLE: Geraldo Greedyperson and you sign a DROA in which Geraldo agrees to sell his Manoa property and you agree to purchase the property for $300,000. You carry out all the terms and conditions of the DROA, but Geraldo gets a higher offer to purchase his property. Geraldo tells you that unless you match the price of the second offer, he will not go through with the sale of his property. You file a lawsuit against Geraldo for specific performance. In court, the judge will determine if the contract you signed with Geraldo is valid and legal and also whether it is just and reasonable. The judge will also determine whether Geraldo has any valid defenses against the lawsuit. If the judge rules in your favor, Geraldo will be ordered to deliver title to you as specified in the DROA.

(3) The buyer may hold the seller responsible for any cost incurred relative to the contract.

The DROA also provides that the foregoing remedies do not exclude any other remedies that are available to either the seller or the buyer. Thus, for instance, although specific performance is available only to the buyer in the foregoing remedies, the seller may also sue for specific performance, as a matter of law. Furthermore, the DROA provides that in case of a lawsuit, the prevailing party is entitled to recover all costs incurred in the lawsuit including reasonable attorney's fees. In addition, all expenses incurred by escrow are deducted from the deposits paid by the buyer before any disbursement is made to the prevailing party.

> IMPORTANT POINT: Should there be a breach of contract, you should contact an attorney immediately not only to find out the remedies available to you, but also because timing may be critical in certain cases. For instance, the buyer's loan commitment may expire on a stipulated date, and the buyer may find himself without a loan to purchase the property. Each case is different, and in order for the attorney to assist you properly, it may be necessary to discover the facts of the dispute and research the law related to your case. A breach of contract is not something to take lightly. You need professional advice to protect your rights.

20 How Is Land Use Regulated?

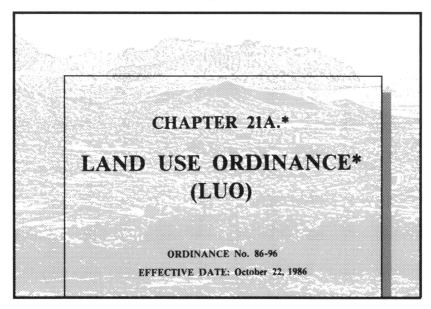

CHAPTER 21A.*

LAND USE ORDINANCE*
(LUO)

ORDINANCE No. 86-96
EFFECTIVE DATE: October 22, 1986

As the owner of land, you do not have an unrestricted right to use your property in whatever manner you please. In 1926, the United States Supreme Court held that it is constitutionally permissible to restrict and control the use of real property by zoning.[15] Regulation is justified as an exercise of the state police power to promote public health, safety, morals, or general welfare. Hawaii's land use laws are complex and complicated, with both the state and counties regulating the use of land. The land owner should take particular care in consulting an expert, such as an attorney, architect, or land planner, if a question should arise in the use of a property.

State Land Use

In 1961, the State Land Use Law (Act 187) was enacted by the legislature, motivated by a need to preserve prime agricultural land, especially on Oahu. Act 187 directed that all Hawaii land be divided into districts. Thus, all lands in the state are currently placed under one of four land use districts: (1) urban, (2) rural, (3) agricultural, and (4) conservation.

A State Land Use Commission was created in 1963 to set standards for determining the boundaries of each district, to determine such boundaries, and to hear and decide petitions for amendments to district boundaries, that is, requests for reclassification (boundary changes). Without question, the State Land Use Commission is one of the most powerful state commissions, because its decisions affect how land may be used. The statute provides that the State Land Use Commission consider the following factors in the determination of the land use districts: (1) For urban districts, lands that are now in urban use and a sufficient reserve area for foreseeable urban growth are to be included. (2) For rural districts, areas of land composed primarily of small farms mixed with very low density residential lots (having a minimum density of not more than one house per one-half acre and a minimum lot size of not less than one-half acre) are to be included. (3) The greatest possible protection is to be given to those lands with a high capacity for intensive cultivation in the establishment of agricultural districts. (4) Forest and water reserve zones are to be included in conservation districts.

The control of land use is exercised as follows:

District	Controlled by
Urban	County
Conservation	State
Agricultural and Rural	Split between state and county

In most instances, petitions for district boundary amendments involving land areas greater than fifteen acres are processed by the State Land Use Commission. Lands of less than fifteen acres are processed by the appropriate land use authority of the county in which the land is situated.

County Zoning Regulations

On the county level, zoning is one of the chief means of regulating land use. All lands other than lands in the state conservation district are subject to county zoning. Zoning is accomplished within the framework of a long-range, comprehensive general plan prepared to guide the overall future development of the county. Zoning is a tool available to the county to put the general plan into effect in an orderly manner. Each county has a zoning map showing all the land and designating the districts in which the land falls. Zoning ordinances both divide land into districts and, within each district, list the permitted uses and regulate the purpose for which structures may be constructed, the height and bulk of the structures, the area of the lot they may occupy, and the number of persons that each lot can accommodate. The permitted uses may also include accessory, temporary, special, or conditional uses.

In the City and County of Honolulu, the following zoning districts have been established, with each district having its own regulations: (1) preservation, (2) agricultural, (3) country, (4) residential, (5) apartment, (6) apartment mixed use, (7) resort, (8) business, (9) business mixed use, (10) industrial, and (11) industrial-commercial mixed use. In addition, certain areas of the City and County of Honolulu have been designated special districts. Within the special districts, there are regulations controlling the development of the land that may not be found in other similarly situated lands. The special districts are (1) the flood hazard district, (2) the Hawaii Capital District, (3) the Diamond Head District, (4) the Punchbowl District, (5) the Chinatown District, (6) the Thomas Square/Honolulu Academy of Arts District, (7) the Waikiki District, and (8) the Haleiwa District.

The zoning ordinances of each county are contained in the following sources:

1. City and County of Honolulu: *Land Use Ordinance,* Ordinance No. 86-96, effective October 22, 1986.

2. County of Hawaii: *Hawaii County Code,* Chapter 25.

3. County of Maui: *Code of the Maui County* (1980), Title 19.28, "Zoning."

4. County of Kauai: *Revised Code of Ordinances of the County of Kauai* (1976), Title IV, Ordinance 164, "County Planning and Land Development."

Other ordinances and rules and regulations that in conjunction with the zoning ordinance, control the use of land and how the land is to be improved include the building code, the subdivision ordinance, and environmental protection laws. Before a land owner can erect a residential structure on his property, he or she must submit proposed building plans to the county building department for approval. A building permit to construct the residential structure will be issued only if the plans comply with the county structural requirements set forth in the building code and the land use restrictions imposed by the zoning ordinance. The building code establishes minimum acceptable material and construction standards for the size of the structure, electrical installations, plumbing, and lighting. Upon completion of the structure, a certificate of occupancy is issued to the owner only if it is constructed in accordance with the building code. It cannot be legally occupied without the certificate.

When a property owner seeks a departure from the zoning requirements (a *variance*), three or four options are available, depending on what type of change is sought. The ordinance of each county determines whether the body or agency to hear and decide the request will be (1) a local legislative body, such as the city council or county council, (2) the administrative zoning office, (3) the zoning board of appeals, or (4) the planning commission. In Honolulu, the agency is the Department of Land Utilization. Generally, under each of the county ordinances, a variance is granted in cases of unnecessary hardship, provided you can show (1) you would be deprived of the reasonable use of your land or building if it were used only for the purpose allowed in that zone; (2) your request is due to unique circumstances and not the general conditions in the neighborhood, so that the reasonableness of the neighborhood zoning is not drawn into question; and (3) the use sought to be authorized by the variance will not alter the essential character of the locality or be contrary to the intent and purpose of the zoning ordinance.

IMPORTANT POINT: The Hawaii land use regulations comprise a maze of numerous and overlapping laws to which an entire book could be devoted. This chapter has provided only a basic introduction to the complex situation facing the land owner. Before purchasing land on which to construct a home or before renovating an existing home, be sure that you or your architect discuss the project with the appropriate county agency to determine whether such construction or renovation is allowed under the existing laws.

21 Should You Insure Your Property?

As the owner of real estate, you are exposed to financial risks. A catastrophe, such as fire, hurricane, flood, or high waves and tsunami (tidal wave), could damage or even destroy your property. A friend, guest, or someone whom you have invited onto your premises—a plumber, electrician, or gardener—may slip and fall and be hurt. The person sustaining an injury may hold you responsible for causing the injury. The customary practice in protecting yourself from any resulting financial loss is to obtain insurance. This is a prudent way of protecting yourself against a hazard or peril. Should there be a mortgage on your property, the financial institution making a loan to you will generally require certain types of insurance.

Property Damage

Most property insurance policies cover loss by fire, but to be covered the damage must be caused by flames. Smoke or heat damage without flames, no matter how severe, generally does not qualify for protection. Furthermore, the fire must be hostile rather than "friendly."

EXAMPLE: Friendly fire is fire burning in a place designed for it. Fire in a fireplace, gas range, or water heater is friendly fire. However, if friendly fire burns out of control, it is then classified as hostile fire, and the insurance company is obligated to pay on the homeowner's claim. If, for instance, the pilot fire in the water heater were to ignite a material in the heater, then this fire would qualify as hostile fire.

Other possible causes of property damage that may be covered in Hawaii include windstorm or hail, explosion, aircraft, vehicles, vandalism, and riots. Coverage for each such additional peril or hazard can be obtained in the form of an *endorsement,* which is also called a *rider* to the basic policy.

It is important that you read your policy carefully to determine against what types of hazard or peril your home is protected. For instance, some insurance will protect your home against wind damage but not against high waves or tsunamis.

Public Liability Insurance

Public liability insurance covers you when you are liable for causing injury to an innocent party by failing to exercise reasonable care. A property owner is responsible for payment for the injuries suffered by the innocent party.

EXAMPLE: You have a legal duty to everyone you invite onto your property (the invitees) to keep the walkway from the sidewalk to your home free and clear of obstructions. After watering your front lawn, you leave the hose on the walkway. The newspaper carrier comes collecting the monthly subscription bill at night, and he stumbles on the hose, falling and injuring his foot. You are liable to the newspaper carrier for the injury he sustains on account of your negligence.

In the area of public liability insurance, it is particularly important that you consult with an insurance agent to determine what coverage will be adequate to protect yourself against the risk of a claim or lawsuit. Bear in mind that in the event of a lawsuit, if judgment is rendered against you, the person suing you may be able to execute your property if your insurance is insufficient to pay the entire judgment.

Homeowner's Policy

The most widely used insurance by owners of homes is the *homeowner's insurance policy,* which is a package policy developed by insurance companies to include coverage of the perils deemed most useful by the insurance experts. Such a policy avoids the overlap of different kinds of insurance and lessens the chance for a gap in coverage. It also costs less to purchase a package policy than to purchase separate individual policies. The homeowner's policy includes both property damage and public liability coverage. The policy may also include coverage for burglary and theft of the homeowner's personal properties. There are as many different kinds of homeowner's policies as there are insurance companies. No one package is right for all homeowners. It is best to discuss the different options available with your insurance agent.

Flood Insurance

In 1968, Congress enacted the National Flood Insurance Program, a joint effort by the insurance industry and the federal government to offer property owners protection for losses to real and personal property resulting from inundation of normally dry areas caused by (1) overflow of inland or tidal waters, (2) unusual and rapid accumulation or runoff of surface waters, (3) mud slides resulting from accumulation of water on or under the ground, and (4) erosion losses caused by abnormal water runoff. All mortgages in which the federal government is involved require either a certificate stating that the mortgaged property is not in a flood zone or a policy of flood insurance. The Federal Housing Administration (FHA), Veterans Administration (VA), and federally insured (FDIC and FSLIC) lenders all require either the certificate or the insurance.

Often in real estate transactions, buyers ask whether they can assume sellers' existing insurance policies. To be sure that you, the buyer, are covered and to prevent a gap in coverage, you should obtain an endorsement from the insurance carrier accepting you as the new policy holder before the closing of the transaction. Without the endorsement, the insurance carrier has no legal responsibility to protect you if an accident occurs after title has passed to you from the seller. The insurance policy protects the real estate owner's insurable interest in the property and not the property itself. In other words, the insurance only protects the owner's interest in the property. If you are unable to obtain an endorsement from the seller's insurance carrier, it is best to obtain your own insurance protection before the closing.

EXAMPLE: Larry "Tomorrow" Lax is advised by his real estate broker to obtain homeowner's insurance coverage before closing. Larry tells his broker not to worry, he will take care of it. A few days after the closing, the house burns down. Larry forgot to talk to his insurance agent about the homeowner's insurance policy. Larry must now assume the total cost of the loss himself.

IMPORTANT POINT: To be prudent it is necessary not only to obtain adequate insurance coverage to protect your home and investment, but you should also periodically review your insurance coverage with your insurance agent. As the value of your property rises and as you add to the personal contents in the residence, it may be necessary to increase your coverage to keep up with the rising valuation.

22 To Lease or Not to Lease?

An understanding of leases is particularly important in Hawaii for several reasons. First, many of the properties on which homeowners reside are located on land owned by huge estates that lease their properties to homeowners for a long term, such as fifty-five years or more. The largest of the estates is the Princess Bernice Pauahi Bishop Estate, whose land holdings in Hawaii are extensive, including commercial as well as residential properties. Second, investment properties owned by private individuals are usually rented to other individuals. Hawaii properties are expensive and a substantial investment for the average person. The property owner should be aware of the rights and responsibilities of a landlord in order to protect his or her investment.

Elements of a Lease Agreement

The lessor (landlord) by means of a lease conveys to the lessee (tenant) the right to possess and use the lessor's property for a specific

138

period of time called the *term*. At the end of the term, the lessor has the right to retake possession of the property. During the lease term, the lessee's right to occupy the property is referred to as a *leasehold estate*.

Because the lease agreement is a contract as well as a conveyance (transfer of real estate interest), it must contain the usual elements of a valid agreement. In the case of a lease, the following are critical: (1) the names of the lessor and the lessee, (2) the location and a description of the leased property, (3) a promise by the lessor to convey the property to the lessee and a promise by the lessee to accept possession of the property, (4) provisions regarding the payment of rent, (5) the starting and expiration dates of the lease (the term), (6) statement of the right to quiet enjoyment by the lessee (the right to use the property without interference by the lessor), (7) indication of the amount of the security deposit, if any, (8) provisions with regard to the payment of utilities, real property taxes, and insurance, and (9) the signatures of the lessor and the lessee.

The lease agreement being a contract, the rules of law that apply to a contract are equally applicable to the lease agreement. Therefore, although the lease relates to real estate, contract law is applied when legal issues arise in the interpretation of the terms and provisions of a lease.

Hawaii Land Reform Act

In 1967, the Hawaii Land Reform Act was enacted as a result of the legislative findings that:

> There is a concentration of land ownership in the State in the hands of a few landowners who have refused to sell the fee simple titles to their lands and who have instead engaged in the practice of leasing their lands under long-term leases;
>
> The refusal of such landowners to sell the fee simple titles to their lands and proliferation of such practice of leasing rather than selling land has resulted in a serious shortage of fee simple residential land and in an artificial inflation of residential land values in the State;
>
> Due to such shortage of fee simple residential land and such artificial inflation of residential land values, the people of the State have been deprived of a choice to own or take a lease of the land on which their

homes are situated and have been required instead to accept long-term leases of such land which contain terms and conditions that are finan-cially disadvantageous, that restrict their freedom to fully enjoy such land and that are weighted heavily in favor of the few landowners of such land;

The acquisition of residential land in fee simple, absolute or other-wise, at fair and reasonable prices by people who are lessees under long-term leases of such land and on which such land their homes are situated and the ability of such people to fully enjoy such land through owner-ship of such land in fee simple will alleviate these conditions and will promote the economy of the State and public interest, health, welfare, security, and happiness of the people of the State.[16]

The law authorizes the Hawaii Housing Authority (HHA) to condemn development tracts, which are residential subdivisions not less than five acres in size, for the acquisition by residents of leased fee interests in residential lots after twenty-five or more lessees, or more than 50 percent of the lessees of residential lease lots, which-ever number is lower, apply to HHA to purchase the leased fee interest. The leased fee interest means all of the interest of the owner in the land leased to the lessee. HHA may designate all or a portion of the development tract for acquisition, depending on the number of lessees applying to HHA. Within twelve months after HHA des-ignates the area in the tract for acquisition, it must acquire the desig-nated area by voluntary action of the parties involved, or it must start eminent domain proceedings to condemn the area. If the des-ignated area is not acquired and no eminent proceedings are insti-tuted, HHA is required to reimburse the fee owner, the lessor, and the legal owners of the property for out-of-pocket expenses they may have incurred.

Among other qualifications, a fee purchaser (1) must be at least 18 years old, (2) must be a bona fide Hawaii resident or have a bona fide intent to reside in the development tract if successful in purchasing the lot, (3) must have legal title to the residential struc-ture on the leased lot, and (4) must have some proof showing that the lessee will be able to pay HHA promptly for the leased fee inter-est in the land.

The lessees have the right to form or join associations to acquire the leased fee interest, to assist each other in forming associations, or to select representatives to bargain with their lessor. The statute specifically provides that neither the lessor nor the organization of lessees shall refuse to bargain in good faith with each other. Communities which have elected to exercise their rights under the statute have in fact formed organizations to bargain with the lessors. Portions of Hawaii Kai, Kahala, and Waialae Iki have organized and successfully acquired leased fee interests from Bishop Estate.

Legal challenges to the Hawaii Land Reform Act by one of Hawaii's major lessors have gone all the way to the United States Supreme Court, which validated the constitutionality of the legislation. Since its inception, the act has facilitated the acquisition of leased fee interests by lessees considerably.

Residential Landlord-Tenant Code

Hawaii's Residential Landlord-Tenant Code governs the rights, remedies, and obligations of the landlord and tenant of any residential rental agreement involving a dwelling unit within the state. It covers rent, limitations on rental agreements and practices, the landlord's obligations, the tenant's obligations, and remedies and penalties. Some of the more important features of the code are the following:

1. A provision in a rental agreement exempting or limiting the landlord, or requiring the tenant to indemnify the landlord from liability for damages to person or property caused by or resulting from the acts or omission of the landlord or his or her agents, servants, or employees is void.

2. A landlord who contemplates converting a rental unit to a condominium must provide notice of at least 120 days before terminating the rental agreement.

3. The landlord must make all repairs and arrangements necessary to put and keep the premises in a habitable condition.

4. The landlord must maintain all electrical, plumbing, and other facilities and appliances supplied by the landlord in good working order and condition.

5. Except in the case of a single-family residence, the landlord must provide receptacles for the removal of normal amounts of rub-

bish and garbage, and arrange for the frequent removal of such
waste material.

6. The landlord and tenant may agree that the tenant shall perform specified repairs, maintenance, and minor remodeling if the
agreement is entered into in good faith and is not intended to evade
the landlord's obligations.

7. The security deposit cannot be construed as payment of the
last month's rent by the tenant.

Most of the provisions that need to be included in a residential
lease agreement are found in the Honolulu Board of Realtors lease
agreement form, which is available to members of that organization.
Landlords who are not members may need to consult an attorney to
prepare a valid, enforceable contract.

The code seems to have been designed largely to protect the tenant. Any technical violation of a code requirement could result in a
lawsuit brought by the tenant against the landlord. The courts
strictly enforce all code requirements, without regard for good faith
efforts on the part of the landlord to abide by the code. As landlord,
moreover, you may find yourself with tenants who are in arrears in
the payment of their rent. Unless you fully comply with the code,
you may find yourself in a lawsuit because of a technical violation of
the code.

Fair Housing Laws

The purpose of the federal and state Fair Housing Laws is to eliminate discrimination in the sale or rental of housing. If there is a conflict between federal law and state law, in most instances the stricter
law prevails.

Two federal laws deal with discrimination in housing. One is the
Civil Rights Act of 1866, which prohibits racial discrimination. In
1968, the United States Supreme Court affirmed that the 1866 Act
prohibits "all racial discrimination, private as well as public, in the
sale of real property.[17] The other federal law is the Fair Housing Act
of 1968, which prohibits discrimination in the sale or rental of housing on the basis of race, color, religion, or national origin. The 1968
law also made it illegal to discriminate because of sex, handicap, or

financial status. However, the 1968 federal law provides a limited number of exceptions: (1) An individual owner selling a house can discriminate, except against race, if the owner (a) does not own more than three dwellings, and (b) has had only one sale in twenty-four months; and (2) for rental units, an owner who occupies a unit in a dwelling for no more than four families can discriminate in selecting tenants for the other three units. However, the Hawaii law restricts the allowability of discrimination to two family units.

If a person believes that he or she has been discriminated against in the sale or rental of housing, a lawsuit may be filed in the federal court for enforcement of the 1866 Act, a complaint may be registered with the Department of Housing and Urban Development, or an action may be filed in the federal district court or a complaint filed with the U.S. Attorney General for enforcement of the 1968 Act.

In Hawaii, state law prohibits discrimination in real property transactions because of race, sex, color, religion, marital status, parental status, ancestry, or a physical handicap. This law, however, does not apply to (1) the rental of a housing accommodation in a building that contains housing accommodations for not more than two families living independently of each other if the lessor or a member of his or her family resides in one of the accommodations; or (2) the rental of a room or rooms in a housing accommodation by an individual if the individual or a member of his or her family resides in the housing.

IMPORTANT POINT: Laws relating to the relationship between landlord and tenant are constantly changing, usually to protect the tenant. To safeguard your rights as a landlord, you must conscientiously abide by all technical requirements.

REFERENCES: Hawaii Land Reform Act. Chapter 516, *Hawaii Revised Statutes*. Residential Landlord-Tenant Code. Chapter 521, *Hawaii Revised Statutes*. Federal Fair Housing Act. Title VIII of the Civil Rights Act of 1968. Real Property Discrimination. Chapter 515, *Hawaii Revised Statutes*.

23 What Are Your Rights When Your Property Is Condemned?

The *Hawaii Constitution* provides that "private property shall not be taken or damaged for public use without just compensation."[18] The Hawaii statute requires that acquisition of private property must be for public use. The power conferred upon the state or counties, referred to as the condemning authority, is called *eminent domain*. Private properties have been condemned for roads, parks, and schools. Property that is taken by a county may be given, sold, set aside or transferred to a private nonprofit organization dedicated to the care of aged persons, so long as it is used for the care of aged persons, among other purposes. The right of eminent domain is also granted to any person or company operating a public utility and engaged in the transportation of passengers or freight. Property that may be taken includes all real estate belonging to any person together with all structures and improvements on the property, water, water rights, and easements.

Legal action to condemn private property is commenced by filing a complaint and issuing a summons to all owners or claimants of the property. The complaint must mention the use to which the property is to be put and contain a description of the property to be condemned and a statement of whether the condemned property includes the whole or only a part of an entire tract or parcel. A map must accompany the complaint correctly delineating the land to be condemned and its location.

In fixing the compensation or damages for the condemned property, the value of the property with all improvements on it is assessed. If any of the improvements are owned by separate owners, their value must be assessed separately. If the condemned property is a portion of a larger tract, the damages to the portion not condemned that will result from the severance of the property, and the construction of the improvements by the state or county are also assessed. Any benefit to the portion not condemned that will accrue from the construction of the improvement is also assessed. The benefit is deducted from the amount of the damages in determining the amount to be awarded as compensation. If the benefit is equal to the amount of damages, then the owner is allowed no compensation.

The amount of the compensation or damages accrues from the date of the summons, and the actual value at that date is the measure of valuation of all property to be condemned. Any improvements put on the property after the date of service of the summons are not included in the assessment of compensation or damages. The condemning authority is required to pay the compensation or damages within two years after the final judgment. If the state or county fails to pay as required, all rights that the state or county may have obtained by the judgment are lost. If the payment is delayed more than thirty days after final judgment, interest at the rate of 5 percent per year is added to the judgment.

When there is a dispute in condemnation cases, it usually centers around the fair market value of the property being condemned. Such a dispute may take several years to resolve and involve prolonged litigation, particularly if the fair market value of the condemning authority and the property owner are far apart. The process becomes a battle of appraisers, with each side presenting its valuation for the judge's decision.

IMPORTANT POINT: Condemnation is actually a complex process. Generally, the more valuable your property, the longer it will take to resolve your claim against the condemning authority.

REFERENCE: Eminent Domain. Chapter 101, *Hawaii Revised Statues*.

24 What Happens When Your Property Is Foreclosed?

NOTICE OF FORECLOSURE
9999 PALOLO AVENUE   HONOLULU, HI
FEE SIMPLE   5,649 SQ.FT.   TMK: 3-4-099-999
Two story masonry/wooden structure, 3 bdrms, 1 bath, living/
kitchen on each level. Approx. 8__ __ft. living ar__ __ch level.
Open garage 320 sq.ft.

OPEN HOUSES: SUNDAY
                  SUNDAY OC__
AUCTION DATE: TUESDAY

If you obtain a loan to pay for your real property, the lender (mortgagee) will require you, as the borrower (mortgagor), to sign a mortgage document in which the lender takes the property as collateral to secure the repayment of a loan. Should you fail to make the required payments, the lender has a right to *foreclose* on the mortgage, to terminate your rights in the property as the borrower.

The lender starts the court proceeding called the *mortgage foreclosure proceeding* by filing a complaint to foreclose on the mortgage. The complaint will name the borrower and refer to the address at which the borrower resides. The address enables the court to determine jurisdiction over the borrower. The complaint is filed in the judicial circuit where the borrower resides and not where the property is located.

> EXAMPLE: The mortgaged real property is located in Kapaa, Kauai, although you reside in Pearl City; the mortgage foreclosure proceeding is filed on Oahu, which is the first circuit.

The complaint also contains the following information: (1) the amount of the loan, (2) the delinquent amount, (3) the terms and conditions of the promissory note and the mortgage, (4) a description of the real property given as collateral, (5) a statement that the lender has a right to foreclose on the property, and (6) a request by the lender that the property be foreclosed, the amount due and owing to the lender be determined by the court, a commissioner be appointed to sell the property by auction, and the sale of the property be confirmed by the court.

The borrower has twenty days to answer the complaint after being served. If the borrower fails to answer the complaint within the twenty days, the lender may file a motion with the court to enter default against the borrower and to take a default judgment for the amount owed to the lender, including all costs, fees, and expenses. When a foreclosure matter is brought before the court, it is heard only by the judge, who decides all factual disputes. No jury is involved.

In the case that there is more than one mortgage on a property, the mortgage lenders are entitled to payment according to the priority of their liens and not by pro rata (proportionate) distribution. A foreclosure of one mortgage extinguishes a subsequent mortgage.

EXAMPLE: Michael and Mildred Easystreet purchase a condominium for $400,000, making a down payment of $100,000. They obtain a first mortgage of $250,000 from Bank of Sandwich Islands and a second mortgage of $50,000 from Universal Bank of U.S.A.

After a year or so, they are unable to make their monthly payments on both the first and second mortgages. The first mortgagee, Bank of Sandwich Islands, files a complaint to foreclose on its first mortgage. Its complaint also names Universal Bank of U.S.A. as defendant, because Universal Bank also has an interest in the property. At the auction, the highest bid is $245,000, which is insufficient to pay off the first mortgage and certainly not enough for the second mortgage. At the confirmation of sale hearing, the court, being advised that $245,000 is the best possible price, will confirm the sale and order that the $245,000 less attorney's fees, commissioner's fees, costs, and expenses be paid to the first mortgagee. The foreclosure extinguishes the second mortgage held by the Universal Bank. In other words, the lien of the second mortgage on the property is cancelled by the foreclosure. If the bid price had been sufficient to pay off both the first and second mortgages and there were still monies remaining after payment to both mortgagees, the balance would be paid to Michael and Mildred Easystreet, the borrower.

The statute requires the mortgagee that intends to foreclose on the mortgage and sell the mortgaged property to give notice by publication once a week for three successive weeks, with the last publication being not less than fourteen days before the date of sale, in a newspaper of general circulation in the county in which the property is located.

In case the mortgaged property is a condominium, the lender is required to notify, by registered or certified mail, the association of apartment owners of the condominium in which the apartment is located of its intent to foreclose.

In instances when the buyer defaults on an agreement of sale and the seller subsequently cancels the agreement, the seller follows the same procedure as in the mortgage foreclosure proceeding.

At the auction, customarily held at a courthouse, the successful bidder is generally required to pay at least 10 percent of the total bid price by certified or cashier's check to the commissioner. The balance must be paid when the court confirms the sale. After the sale by auction is confirmed by the court, when the successful bidder pays in full for the property, the commissioner appointed by the court to sell the foreclosed property delivers a commissioner's deed to the bidder. The successful bidder derives right, title, and interest in the property from the commissioner, not from the owners whose property had been foreclosed. Once a property is foreclosed, the owner no longer has any right in the property to transfer to another person.

IMPORTANT POINT: If you are unable to make your mortgage payments, as a practical matter, rather than having your property foreclosed, you should ask your lender for sufficient time to sell your property. You might be able to sell the property for a profit, thereby enabling you to pay off your mortgage and avoiding additional expenses, such as court costs and attorney's fees.

REFERENCE: Mortgage Foreclosures. Chapter 667, *Hawaii Revised Statutes*.

25 What Happens to Your Property When You Die?

```
                 LAST WILL AND TESTAMENT

                           OF

                      MAKE D. DEAD



KNOW ALL MEN BY THESE PRESENTS:

    I, MAKE D. DEAD, of Mililani, State of Hawaii, declare

this my Will and revoke all prior wills and codicils made by

me.

    ONE: I direct that there be paid out of my residuary

estate and out of funds received from the Trustee under my

trust instrument executed this date, my funeral and
```

When a person dies owning real estate, certain questions are raised: Who is entitled to the decedent's (deceased person's) right, title, and interest in the real estate? What is required to transfer the decedent's ownership to beneficiaries or heirs? Is the government entitled to the property if the decedent dies without a will? Must the decedent's family report the death to any government agency or office? The answers to these and other questions depend on how the decedent held the property at the time of death.

Earlier chapters have shown that real estate can be held solely in the owner's name or jointly with another person or persons (tenancy by the entirety, joint tenancy, and tenancy in common), or an owner may be a stockholder in a corporation that holds the title in the real estate, or a partner in a general or limited partnership holding the title in the partnership name, or a beneficiary of a trust.

Real Estate Owned Individually

One of the biggest advantages of owning real estate solely in your name is that you have absolute control over the property without being accountable to any other person. As the individual owner, you have the right to manage or use your property in whatever way you desire. The disadvantage of holding real estate solely in your name is that when you die, it is necessary to transfer your right, title, and interest in the real estate, like any personal property held solely in your name, by a judge through a judicial proceeding commonly referred to as a "probate proceeding." Technically, *probate* means to offer as proof a decedent's instrument (document) as the decedent's last will and testament. However, when reference is made to the need to probate property, it is generally understood to mean that it is necessary for the court to transfer title to the property by a judicial proceeding.

If the decedent dies owning real property solely in the decedent's name, it is necessary to probate the property whether the person dies with or without a will. The tenancy on the property determines whether it is necessary to probate the property. If there is a will, the *testator* (a male person making a will) or *testatrix* (a female person making a will) by his or her will stipulates the beneficiaries of his or her properties. If a person owning real property in Hawaii dies without a will (intestate), the Hawaii statute known as the *law of intestacy* determines the beneficiaries and the share that each beneficiary receives in the distribution of the probate assets.[19] When a testator or testatrix draws up a will, he or she decides whom the beneficiaries are to be and the share that each beneficiary will receive under the will. In the case of a person dying without a will, the law of intestacy decides for the decedent who the beneficiaries will be and the share that each beneficiary will take, regardless of whether or not the decedent intended to bequeath any share to a particular person entitled to receive under the law of intestacy.

Under the law of intestacy, if the decedent dies leaving a surviving spouse, and if there are no lineal (direct) descendants or parents of the decedent, the spouse is entitled to the entire estate. If there are surviving lineal descendants or parents of the decedent, the spouse is entitled to one-half of the estate.

EXAMPLE: Matt Make dies, leaving a spendthrift son, Spendo, and a hard-working, long-suffering wife, Faith. He did not make a will. Under the law of intestacy, Faith is entitled to only one-half of the estate and Spendo is entitled to the other half, although Matt may have chosen not to leave anything to Spendo if he had made a will before he died.

If the decedent dies without a surviving spouse, the estate passes (1) to the lineal descendants. If they are all of the same degree of kinship, they all take equally; if of unequal degree, those of remote degree take by representation (that is, they take what their parent would have taken). (2) If there are no lineal descendants, the estate passes to the decedent's parents equally. (3) If there are no surviving lineal descendants or parents, the estate passes to the lineal descendants of the parents. The statute goes on to name other beneficiaries if there are no surviving lineal descendants, parents, lineal descendants of parents, grandparents, or great-grandparents. It is only after there is no taker under the law of intestacy that the intestate estate passes to the state. This taking is referred to as *escheat*.

One of the advantages of drawing up a will is the right of the testator to designate his beneficiaries. However, in Hawaii, a property owner may not disinherit his or her spouse of real estate. The law provides that if a married person domiciled (residing) in the state dies, leaving a spouse surviving, the spouse has a *right of election* to take an *elective share* of one-third of the net estate. This right also belongs to the surviving spouse of a married person not domiciled in Hawaii with real property in the state.[20] However, if a married person not domiciled in the state dies leaving personal property, the right of the surviving spouse to an elective share of the personal property (if any) is governed by the law of the state that is the decedent's domicile at death.

If there is a probate proceeding, to complete the administration of the estate before the assets can be distributed to the beneficiaries, a report from the State of Hawaii Department of Taxation indicating whether state estate taxes have been paid must be filed with the probate court. In order to receive a report, it is necessary to file a State of Hawaii estate tax return disclosing all of the assets of the decedent.

At the very end of the probate process, the probate judge will enter an "order approving final accounts, settling estate, and distributing estate," by which title to any real estate is *vested* by the court to the beneficiaries, subject to all encumbrances, liens, and mortgages on the property. In this context, vested means that title is fixed or settled by the court in the beneficiaries. The probate judge does not transfer the interest of the decedent to the beneficiaries by deed. The order then must be recorded with the Bureau of Conveyances. It is by this recordation that the real property tax official of each county is made aware of the change in ownership from the decedent to the beneficiary or beneficiaries. In the case of individually owned real estate, the mere reporting of the death of the property owner to the tax office does not mean that the title is automatically transferred from the sole owner to the beneficiaries. It is necessary to probate the decedent's solely owned property.

Jointly Owned Real Estate

In chapter 14, you were informed that real estate can be owned jointly in three ways: tenancy by the entirety, joint tenancy, and tenancy in common. Inherent in both tenancy by the entirety—ownership by a husband and wife—and joint tenancy is a *right of survivorship,* which means that upon the death of one owner, the interest of the decedent devolves (passes on) automatically to the surviving owner of the property. Because the interest of the decedent is automatically transferred to the surviving owners by operation of law, it is not necessary to probate the interest of the decedent in such cases. It is often asked whether it is necessary to delete the name of the decedent on the deed or other such conveyance instrument. The answer is no, because by law the decedent no longer has any right, title, or interest in the property. If and when the property is sold or otherwise transferred to another party by the surviving owners, the fact that the decedent has died and the date of death are usually mentioned in the conveyance instrument.

> EXAMPLE: "Being the same property conveyed by deed dated May 5, 1955, to the grantor and her husband, Fred Firsttodie, whose interest having devolved to the grantor upon his death on July 13, 1987."

When property is owned as tenancy in common, where there is a distinct interest in the property and no right of survivorship, the interest of the decedent must be probated like a solely owned property.

EXAMPLE: Fred Firsttodie owns a 25 percent interest in a parcel of real estate. On his death, his 25 percent interest in the property will have to be probated and distributed to his beneficiary or beneficiaries as stipulated in his will or, if there is no will, according to the law of intestacy.

Real Estate Owned by a Corporation

Real estate may be owned by a corporation and the title to the property taken in the name of the corporation. A stockholder of the corporation owning the real estate would indirectly own the real estate. Decisions concerning the real estate are in the hands of the board of directors, who make all management and policy decisions for and on behalf of the corporation. Therefore, a stockholder who is not a member of the board of directors does not have a right to participate in the decision-making process. In most instances, stocks can be sold or transferred without much legal problem. One possible restriction is a shareholders' agreement in which all the shareholders agree to offer the stocks for sale first to the corporation or other shareholders, or vice versa, before being permitted to sell the stocks to an outsider.

If a corporation is listed on one of the major stock exchanges in the country, it is easy to sell the stocks. Just contact a stockbroker, who will execute your order to sell your shares of stock with the appropriate stock exchange. It is as simple as a telephone call to the stockbroker. If you are in possession of the stock certificate, you deliver the stock certificate to the broker and instruct her to sell the stock. If the shares of stock are not listed or are in a closely held corporation with few stockholders, you will be required to sign the stock certificate, assigning it to the transferee. Again, this is a simple procedure. In essence, then, the transfer of shares of stock in a corporation, whether large or small, is an uncomplicated procedure.

An advantage in corporate ownership of real estate is that the term of the corporation is perpetual. Unless it is dissolved, the corporation can exist in perpetuity (forever), unlike a human being whose life sooner or later terminates. However, on the death of a shareholder, shares of stock owned solely in the shareholder's name must be probated, and all the probate and tax requirements mentioned earlier are applicable. If the stocks are owned jointly, the rules applicable to jointly owned property come into play.

Real Property Owned by a Partnership

Under Hawaii's partnership laws, real property can be owned and held in the name of a partnership. If the partnership is a *general partnership,* the death of one partner will automatically dissolve the partnership. In a *limited partnership,* one or more persons are general partners with full liability to any creditor, and the other persons are limited partners. The limited partners are usually referred to as *silent partners,* whose role is merely one of investors in the partnership. On the death of a partner, whether a general or limited partner, his interest in the partnership will be probated if it is owned solely by the partner. In this instance, the probate and tax requirements for a solely owned property are applicable. If the partnership interest is held jointly, then the joint ownership rules will govern.

Real Estate Owned by a Trust

In a case in which real estate is owned by a trust, title to the property is held by the trustee, which can be either an individual or a corporation, and the beneficiary possesses an *equitable interest* in the trust. The powers and duties of the trustee are usually set forth in the trust instrument creating the trust. The trustee manages and deals with the real property according to the terms and conditions of the trust instrument. If the real property is sold, purchased, leased, encumbered, or in any way transferred, it is done by the trustee. The beneficiary merely enjoys the income from the real estate or, in some instances, depending on the terms and conditions of the trust instrument, is entitled to dip into the principal of the trust. Often there are special provisions for emergencies or medical or health reasons.

What happens to the beneficiary's interest in the trust when the beneficiary dies depends on the intent of the settlor who created the trust. The intent can be determined by reading the trust instrument. The income of the trust and the trust property, upon the termination of the trust, may be divided among surviving beneficiaries. Or, the beneficiary's interest may be divided and distributed to his or her children, grandchildren, or heirs at law (persons who succeed to the interest of the decedent).

There is no probate when there is a trust. This is the beauty of a trust—it avoids probate. The transfer of any interest in the trust property is done by the trustee, and, because there is no probating of assets, all information relative to the trust property and its beneficiaries remains confidential, unlike a probate in which all information becomes a part of the public records.

In summary, the following require that your interest be probated:

1. Real estate owned in your individual (sole) name.
2. Real estate owned as a tenant in common.
3. Shares of stock in a corporation owning real estate held in your individual name.
4. Partnership interest held in your individual name.

The following types of interest are transferred to the survivor automatically:

1. Tenancy by the entirety (to your spouse).
2. Joint tenancy (to the surviving owner).
3. Any stock in a corporation or any partnership interest held as a tenancy by the entirety or joint tenancy.

The following is transferred to your designated beneficiary or beneficiaries upon your death:

1. Trust created by you. Your trustee transfers the trust property to the beneficiary or beneficiaries you have designated in the trust instrument.

IMPORTANT POINT: In estate planning the question is often asked, "What is the best way to hold property?" There is no one best way applicable across the board for everyone. It depends on your intent. If you wish to control your property to the very end of your life, hold it solely in your name. If you wish to avoid probate, consider joint ownership or setting up a corporation. Think about who in your family you wish to be your beneficiaries, tax considerations, and your ability to manage your real estate in case of illness or incapacity. Again, you are advised to consult an experienced professional who can explain to you the advantages and disadvantages of all alternatives.

REFERENCES: Uniform Probate Code. Title 30A, *Hawaii Revised Statutes*. Land Trusts. Chapter 558, *Hawaii Revised Statutes*.

APPENDIX A

Classes of Real Estate

To really understand the different interests in real property in Hawaii, it is necessary to recognize the influence of English law on the real estate law. The lawyers and jurists who had a hand in the establishment of the American legal system in Hawaii during the Hawaiian monarchy in the 1800s were mostly from New England, where English legal principles and practices were followed to a great extent. Basic Anglo-American real property law in the nineteenth century was a carry-over from the English feudal system, and to this day real property law can be better understood by bearing in mind the feudal system in which the king owned all the land and distributed designated parcels to his vassals for their use and enjoyment.

Frequently, lawyers discussing the different interests in real property will mention the *bundle of rights* held by the owner. This term refers to the numerous rights that a particular owner may have in the specific real property: the greater the number of sticks in the bundle, the higher the class of real property owned. The bundle of rights in the property is also called *estate,* referring to the interest and rights that a person has in real property.

Historically, estates in land were considered either *freehold estates* or *leasehold estates*. The main difference is that disputes involving freehold estates were litigated under real property law, whereas leasehold disputes were tried under personal property law. For an estate to be a freehold estate the person with the interest must actually own the land, and the estate must not be of any set duration. Examples of freehold estates are fee estates, life estates, and estates created by statute. In a leasehold estate, the person holding the land does not own but merely possesses it, and the estate is of a definite duration. The types of freehold and leasehold estates most relevant in Hawaii are discussed below. Some of the other estates in English real property law are archaic and not applicable in modern real estate.

159

Freehold Estates

Fee simple is the largest estate that a person can hold in land. A fee simple interest may be subject to limitations imposed by the person creating the estate. Such estates are referred to as *qualified fee estates,* and they fall into three categories: (1) *fee simple determinable,* (2) *condition subsequent,* and (3) *condition precedent.*

A fee simple determinable estate is a fee simple estate that is limited by the happening of a certain event.

> EXAMPLE: John D. Bigrock conveys a parcel of land on Merchant Street in Honolulu to Peter Pureheart as long as no alcoholic beverage is manufactured or sold on the property. The Merchant Street property will revert back to the grantor, John D. Bigrock (a *reversion*), or to someone designated by the grantor (a *remainderman*) automatically upon the happening of such an event.

A fee simple subject to condition subsequent is similar to a fee simple determinable except that the termination of the fee simple is not automatic. The happening of the event simply gives the grantor the right to terminate the estate. For instance, in the above illustration, John D. Bigrock possesses the right to terminate the fee simple estate if Peter Pureheart or his heirs were to manufacture or sell alcoholic beverages. In order to terminate the estate, the grantor would be required to exercise the right.

Fee simple subject to condition precedent refers to the situation in which the owner would not become vested (possess the ownership rights) with a fee simple estate until an event occurred.

> EXAMPLE: John D. Bigrock conveys the same Merchant Street property to Peter Pureheart on the condition that the land be cleared of rubbish and weeds. When the condition is fulfilled, Peter Pureheart is vested with fee simple title in the property.

Life estate is a fee simple estate that lasts for the life of a person. It can be the life of the person holding the interest (a *life tenant*) or a third person.

EXAMPLE: Pikake Wong may decide to convey Aloha Hale to her son, Kimo, for as long as he shall live, or Pikake Wong can convey Aloha Hale to Kimo for as long as Kimo's wife, Jane, shall be living.

There must be a person named to take the property upon the death of the life tenant.

EXAMPLE: Pikake Wong decides to convey Aloha Hale "to Kimo Wong, for as long as he shall live, and upon his death, to his wife, Jane." On Kimo's death, Jane becomes the owner of Aloha Hale.

To avoid probate and still retain an interest in a property, parents may convey their real property to their child or children and reserve a life interest in the property for their own protection and sense of security. As long as the parents retain a life interest in the property, the children will not be able to evict them from the property. On the death of the parents, since the property is already in the names of the children, probate of the property is avoided, and the children become the full owners of the property automatically.

Leasehold Estates

Under a leasehold estate, the owner of a property is the *lessor*, or landlord, and the person using and enjoying the property is the *lessee*, or tenant. Under the law, as long as the lessee pays the rent and performs all of the terms and conditions of the lease, the lessor cannot use the property or go onto the property—except to inspect the premises to determine whether the lessee is fulfilling the terms and conditions of the lease—until the expiration of the lease term.

The lessor has a right to recover possession of the premises when the lease term expires. During the lease term, the lessor holds a *reversionary interest* in the property, that is, the interest in the property reverts to the lessor at the expiration of the lease.

The four categories of leasehold estates are (1) *estate for years*, (2) *periodic estate*, (3) *estate at will*, and (4) *tenancy at sufferance*. An estate for years, also called *tenancy for years*, has a specific date of commencement of the lease and a specific expiration date. Although the word "years" is used, the lease term need not necessarily be for a term of years. It can be for a number of days or months.

> EXAMPLE: Kimo Big Kala, the land owner, leases Lani Acres to Jane Jones for a term of five years starting January 1, 1990, and ending on December 31, 1994. Then, Jane Jones leases the same property, Lani Acres, to Mahalo Corp. for six months from February 1, 1990, to July 31, 1990. In this case, Kimo Big Kala is the *master lessor,* and Jane Jones acts in a dual capacity: she is both the *master lessee* under her lease with Kimo Big Kala and the *sublessor.* The sublease that Jane Jones has with the land owner, Kimo Big Kala, is commonly referred to as a *sandwich lease.*

Periodic estate, also called the *estate from year to year,* is a lease with a fixed term that unless terminated by either the landlord or the tenant, is renewed for the same term. The term can be less than one year. For example, a month-to-month tenancy continues each month until terminated either by the landlord or the tenant. Estate by will, also called *tenancy at will,* is a landlord-tenant relationship that may be terminated at any time by either the landlord or the tenant. Tenancy at sufferance occurs when the tenant remains on the leased premises beyond the lease term without the consent of the landlord. In this situation, the tenant, referred to as a *holdover tenant,* can be evicted by the landlord at any time after the expiration of the lease term. If the holdover tenant pays rent to the landlord and he or she accepts the rent, the tenancy changes to a periodic tenancy (estate).

Statutory Interest

Besides freehold estates and leasehold estates, there are estates created by law. They include *dower* and *curtesy,* which are no longer applicable in Hawaii. However, any dower or curtesy right that vested prior to July 1, 1977, is still valid. An attorney can help to clarify these matters.

Dower is the right granted to a wife in her husband's property. Until June 30, 1977, the surviving wife's dower included one-third part of all the lands owned by her husband in fee simple, in freehold, or in leasehold at any time during marriage. With the dower right granted to the wife, a husband could not convey all of his property to a third party and leave nothing for his wife. Dower rights, however, were barred by divorce.

Curtesy is the right given to a husband in his wife's property, which until June 30, 1977, included a one-third part of the property owned by her at the date of her death after payment of all her just debts. During the life of his wife, the husband did not have any curtesy right in the wife's property.

Under the Uniform Probate Code, in lieu of dower and curtesy, the statute now provides for an *elective share* for the surviving spouse, as described in chapter 25.

Government Offices

The following are government offices relating to real estate:

Federal Offices

Environmental Protection Agency
Prince Kuhio Federal Building, Room 1302
Honolulu, Hawaii 96813
(808) 541–2710

Farmers' Home Administration
Prince Kuhio Federal Building, Room 3320
Honolulu, Hawaii 96813
(808) 541–2582

Department of Housing and Urban Development
Prince Kuhio Federal Building, Room 3318
Honolulu, Hawaii 96813
Fair Housing and Equal Opportunity Division: (808) 541–1329
Housing Division: (808) 541–1332

U.S. Army Corps of Engineers
Operations Division
Fort Shafter
Honolulu, Hawaii 96819
(808) 438–9258

State Offices

Attorney General
State Capitol
Honolulu, Hawaii 96813
(808) 548–4740

Department of Business and Economic Development
250 S. King Street, Room 610
Honolulu, Hawaii 96813
Coastal Zone Management: (808) 548–8467

165

Department of Commerce and Consumer Affairs
1010 Richards Street
Honolulu, Hawaii 96813
Architects, Engineers, and Surveyors: (808) 548–8542
Business Registration: (808) 548–6111
Condominium Managing Agents: (808) 548–6464
Condominium Registration: (808) 548–3201
Contractors Licensing Board: (808) 548–7637
Electricians and Plumbers: (808) 548–3952
Real Estate Commission: (808) 548–7464
Real Estate Information Officer: (808) 548–7579
Subdivison: (808) 548–7697
Time Sharing: (808) 548–3425

Hawaii Community Development Authority
677 Ala Moana Blvd., Suite 1001
Honolulu, Hawaii 96813
(808) 548–7180

Hawaii Housing Authority
1002 N. School Street
Honolulu, Hawaii 96817
Housing Management Property Manager: (808) 848–3273
Hula Mae: (808) 848–3266
Public Housing Rentals: (808) 848–3277

Department of Land and Natural Resources
1151 Punchbowl Street
Honolulu, Hawaii 96813
Bureau of Conveyances: (808) 548–7416

Land Use Commission
335 Merchant Street, Room 104
Honolulu, Hawaii 96813
(808) 548–4611

City and County of Honolulu Offices

Building Department
650 S. King Street
Honolulu, Hawaii 96813
Permit Section: (808) 523–4505
Building Code Plans Examining: (808) 523–4505

Finance Department
Real Property Assessment Division
842 Bethel Street
Honolulu, Hawaii 96813
(808) 527–5500

General Planning Department
650 S. King St.
Honolulu, Hawaii 96813
General Plan Branch: (808) 527–6066
Planning Commission: (808) 523–4430

Department of Land Utilization
650 S. King Street
Honolulu, Hawaii 96813
(808) 523–4131

Real Property Tax Collections
530 S. King Street
Honolulu, Hawaii 96813
(808) 523–4856

Zoning Board of Appeals
650 S. King Street
Honolulu, Hawaii 96813
(808) 523–4039

County of Hawaii Offices

Finance Department
Real Property Tax Office
865 Piilani Street
Hilo, Hawaii 96827
(808) 961–8201

Planning Department
25 Aupuhi Street
Hilo, Hawaii 96827
(808) 961–8288

County of Kauai Offices

Finance Department
Real Property Tax Division
4280A Rice Street
Lihue, Kauai, Hawaii 96766
(808) 245–7366

Planning Department
4280 Rice Street
Lihue, Kauai, Hawaii 96766
(808) 245–3919

County of Maui Offices

Department of Finance
1580 Kaahumanu Street
Wailuku, Maui, Hawaii 96793
Property Tax Division: (808) 243–7702
Real Property Tax Administrator: (808) 243–7705

Planning Department: (808) 243–7735
Wailuku, Maui, Hawaii 96793

Land Use and Codes Administration
Department of Public Works
200 S. High Street
Wailuku, Maui, Hawaii 96793
Building Permits: (808) 243–7373
Zoning & House Code: (808) 243–7373

APPENDIX C

Sample Forms

This form was prepared by the HAWAII ASSOCIATION OF REALTORS for use by its members.

HAWAII ASSOCIATION OF REALTORS® STANDARD FORMS
DEPOSIT RECEIPT, OFFER AND ACCEPTANCE 9/89 ("DROA")
(The Standard Terms on the Reverse Side are part of the DROA)

REALTOR®

REALTORS and REALTOR-ASSOCIATES are professionals who are members of the NATIONAL ASSOCIATION OF REALTORS® and subscribe to its strict Code of Ethics.
If this transaction involves a sale of property at a price less than $25,000, Hawaii's Plain Language Statute may apply. If so, ATTACH AN EXECUTED PLAIN LANGUAGE ADDENDUM.

Reviewed by: _____
(Principal Broker, Broker in Charge, Authorized Signature)

Reference Date: _____

DEPOSIT RECEIPT

Received from _____ herein called Buyer the sum of $ _____

in the form of _____ as an initial deposit on account of this offer. Receipt is acknowledged by (REALTOR)(REALTOR-Associate) _____

_____ REALTOR'S firm and address _____

PHONES (Bus.) _____ (Home) _____ (FAX) _____

OFFER

1. **PURCHASE PRICE:** _____

2. **PROPERTY DESCRIPTION:** Tax Map Key Division _____ /Zone _____ /Sec _____ /Plat _____ /Parcel _____ /CPR _____

   (a) **Realty:** All of that (leasehold) (fee simple) property situated at _____

   _____ Hawaii, described as follows: _____

   (b) **Seller's Real Property Disclosure Statement** dated _____ (has) (has not) been received by Buyer.
   If not, address in paragraph 8, Special Terms. (b-1) **Residential Leasehold Property Addendum** (is) (is not) made a part of this DROA.

   (c) **Sale Includes:** All built-in furniture, attached fixtures, built-in appliances, water heater, electrical and/or gas and plumbing fixtures, attached carpeting, existing drapes, and the following items if checked: Chandelier ( ); Range ( ); Refrigerator ( ); Disposal ( ); Dishwasher ( ); Compactor ( ); Washer ( ); Dryer ( ); Air Conditioner ( ); TV Antenna ( ); TV Cable Outlet ( ); Ceiling Fan ( ); Furnishings per attached inventory ( ); Pool Equipment ( ); and _____

   Specifically excluded: _____

   (d) **Title:** Seller agrees to convey the property with warranties vesting marketable title in Buyer, free and clear of all liens and encumbrances except _____

   and any other covenants, easements, reservations or restrictions now of record which do not materially affect the value of the property.

   (e) **Assessments:** _____ shall be (paid by Seller at closing) (assumed by Buyer).

3. **FINANCING:** Buyer agrees to pay said purchase price as follows:

   ADDITIONAL DEPOSIT: $ _____ in cash to be made on or before _____ .

   $ _____ in cash at closing including all deposits herein.

   $ _____ by way of _____

   $ _____

   $ _____ Total Purchase Price (see paragraph 1 above)

4. **CLOSING:** Closing will be on or before _____ , 19 _____ . Escrowed by _____ .

5. **OCCUPANCY:** Seller agrees to give Buyer occupancy at closing or on _____ , 19 _____ .

6. **PRORATIONS:** Property taxes, lease rents, interest on assumed obligations, mortgage insurance premiums, other insurance premiums, maintenance fees, tenants' rents, if applicable, and _____ shall be prorated as of the date of closing or on _____ , 19 _____ . Tenants' security deposit, if any, shall be charged to Seller and credited to Buyer at closing.

7. **TENANCY:** Title shall vest in Buyer(s) as follows: _____
   print full legal name(s) and marital status (no initials)

   _____ Tenancy: _____

8. **SPECIAL TERMS:** (Please number) _____

9. **AGENCY DISCLOSURE:** The Buyer is represented by _____ and all its salespeople. The Seller is represented by _____ and all its salespeople. Oral or written disclosure was provided before the signing of this offer.

10. **AGREEMENT TO BUY:** Buyer agrees to buy the property on the terms and conditions contained herein including **The Standard Terms On The Reverse Side**, acknowledges receipt of a copy hereof, and agrees that this offer shall be binding if accepted by Seller before _____ , 19 _____ , _____ AM/PM.

Offer Date _____ , 19 _____ , _____ AM/PM.

Buyer's address: _____

Phones: (Bus.) _____ (Home) _____

Buyer _____
signature
SS# _____

Buyer _____
signature
SS# _____

ACCEPTANCE

11. **AGREEMENT TO SELL:** Seller agrees to sell the property at the price and terms offered above, including **The Standard Terms On The Reverse Side**, and acknowledges that he has been given a copy of this offer.

12. **SELLER'S AGREEMENT TO PAY COMMISSION:** I agree to pay to _____

a commission for the above sale of _____ in U.S. dollars. I hereby instruct escrow to pay your commission directly to you at closing. I agree that I cannot change these instructions without your written consent. Unless otherwise agreed upon, I give you permission to share this commission as you see fit with the real estate company named here in the **DEPOSIT RECEIPT** section of this agreement. In the event of Buyer's default, if I retain the deposit(s), I agree to pay you one half of the amount I retain, but you shall not be paid more than what would have been your full commission.

Date _____ , 19 _____ , _____ AM/PM.

Seller's Name _____
print full legal name
Seller's Tax Identification # to be reported to IRS _____

Seller's Name _____
print full legal name
Seller's Tax Identification # to be reported to IRS _____

Seller's Address _____

Seller's Address _____

Signature _____

Signature _____
Foreign Person ( )   Owner occupant ( )   Other ( )

Phones: (Bus.) _____ (Home) _____

ACKNOWLEDGEMENT OF ACCEPTANCE: The undersigned acknowledges that he has been given a copy of the acceptance of this offer.

Date _____ , 19 _____ , _____ AM/PM.   Signature _____

STANDARD TERMS

A. CONTRACT:

This is more than a receipt for money. It is a legally binding contract. Read it carefully.

B. EVIDENCE OF TITLE:

Seller shall furnish Buyer evidence of Seller's marketable title to the interest which is to be conveyed to Buyer. If Seller fails to deliver title as herein provided, Buyer has the option to terminate this agreement and have any of Buyer's deposits returned to Buyer. The foregoing shall not exclude any other remedies available to Buyer. Buyer will receive an Owner's standard coverage policy of title insurance at closing: (a) Seller shall pay 60% of the premium to be charged for an Owner's standard coverage policy of title insurance to be issued to the Buyer in the amount of the sales price; and, (b) Buyer shall pay 40% of such premium and any additional costs relating to the issuance of any extended coverage policy, including a Lender's policy.

C. STAKING:

Seller shall order and pay for the cost of the staking by a licensed surveyor if stakes are not visible. The Buyer may have a licensed surveyor verify the accuracy of the location of stakes prior to closing and the Seller agrees to reimburse the Buyer for the cost of this staking on or before closing only if the original stakes prove to be inaccurate. This provision does not apply to a condominium or cooperative apartment. (Note: Staking is not a survey and does not confirm the accuracy of the land area description or the absence of encroachments.)

D. CUSTOMARY CLOSING COSTS (Except Where Not Applicable):

These are customary costs and are not intended to be an all inclusive list.

Expenses to be paid by Buyer	**Expenses to be paid by Seller**
Continuation of Title Evidence	Evidence Showing Marketable Title
Title Insurance (As printed in Standard Term B., above)	Title Insurance (As printed in Standard Term B., above)
Drafting of Agreement of Sale	Drafting of Deed or Assignment of Lease
Drafting of Mortgage and Note	Drafting of Bill of Sale
Drafting of Buyer's Consents	Drafting of Seller's Consents
Buyer's Consent Fee	Seller's Consent Fee
Buyer's Notary Fee	Seller's Notary Fee
All Recording Fees except Documents to Clear Seller's Title	Conveyance Tax
½ Escrow Fee	½ Escrow Fee
Condo Ownership Transfer Fee	Staking
FHA Discounts When Applicable	VA or FHA Discount Points When Applicable
Mortgage Assumption Fee	Termite Inspection
	Termite Treatment if Required as per Standard Term E

E. TERMITE INSPECTION:

Seller shall deliver to Buyer through escrow a report from a licensed pest control company stating that there is no live visible termite infestation in the improvements described herein. Seller shall pay for termite extermination treatment if it is required.

F. SELLER'S LIMITED WARRANTY:

Seller warrants and Buyer will acknowledge in writing that all major appliances, plumbing and electrical and/or gas fixtures included in the sale will be in working order consistent with their age as of the date of closing or occupancy, if earlier. No continuing warranty is expressed or implied.

G. RISK OF LOSS:

Risk of loss passes to Buyer upon transfer of title or occupancy whichever occurs first.

H. DEFAULT:

It is expressly understood and agreed: First: In the event Buyer fails to pay the balance of the purchase price or complete the purchase as herein provided, Seller may (a) bring an action for damages for breach of contract; (b) retain the initial deposit and all additional deposits provided for herein, as liquidated damages; and (c) Buyer shall be responsible for any cost incurred in accordance with this contract. Second: In the event Seller fails to perform his obligations as herein provided, Buyer not being in default, Buyer may (a) bring an action against Seller for damages for breach of contract; (b) file and maintain an action against Seller for specific performance of this contract; and (c) Seller shall be responsible for any cost incurred in accordance with this contract. The foregoing shall not exclude any other remedies available to either Seller or Buyer. In the event of default and/or a lawsuit arising out of this contract (including a suit by a REALTOR for commission), the prevailing party shall be entitled to recover all costs incurred including reasonable attorney's fees. All expenses incurred by escrow shall be deducted from deposited funds prior to any disbursement to the prevailing party.

I. CLOSING:

For the purpose of this contract "closing" shall be the date upon which all appropriate documents are recorded. Buyer and Seller agree to execute appropriate or customary documents when requested to do so.

J. CONSENT:

The obligations of Buyer or Seller hereunder are conditioned upon obtaining those necessary consents of vendors, existing mortgagees, lessors and/or condominium, co-op or other such associations; Buyer or Seller agree to cooperate and take all reasonable action to obtain such consents.

K. TIME IS OF THE ESSENCE:

If either Buyer or Seller for reasons beyond his control cannot perform his obligation to purchase or sell the property by the closing date, then such party by giving escrow written notice prior to the closing date called for in this contract with copies to all parties to this contract, can extend closing for no longer than 30 calendar days to allow performance. Thereafter time is of the essence and the default provisions of Standard Term H. apply. Any further extension must then be agreed to in writing by both parties. There is no automatic right to extend. This provision relates only to the extension of the closing date.

L. OBLIGATIONS:

REALTOR shall not be held liable to either Buyer or Seller for the failure of either to perform their obligations pursuant to this contract.

M. CONFLICT:

Handwritten or typed provisions herein shall supersede any printed provisions in this contract if there is a conflict.

N. PERMISSION:

REALTOR has Buyer's and Seller's permission to supply data to the Multiple Listing Service regarding the sales price and terms of this transaction for use by REALTORS in making market studies, providing service to the public and advising their clients.

O. COMPLETE AGREEMENT:

This contract constitutes the entire agreement between Buyer and Seller and supersedes and cancels any and all prior negotiations, representations, warranties, understandings or agreements (both written and oral) of Buyer and Seller. No variation or amendment of this contract shall be valid or enforceable without written approval by Buyer and Seller.

_____   _____
Seller's Initials   Buyer's Initials

IMPORTANT: PLEASE SEPARATE DROA COPIES BEFORE EXECUTING COOPERATING REALTOR'S SEPARATE AGREEMENT OR SIGNATURES WILL COPY THROUGH TO OTHER SIDE.

COOPERATING REALTOR'S SEPARATE AGREEMENT

Seller's REALTOR agrees to pay to Cooperating REALTOR through escrow at closing the following amount: _____
in consideration of assistance given by Cooperating REALTOR. In the event Seller retains Buyer's deposit money as liquidated damages and Seller's REALTOR retains a portion of the deposit as stated in paragraph 12, Seller's REALTOR will share ½ of his retained funds with Cooperating REALTOR.

Date_____ , 19 _____   Date_____ , 19 _____

Seller's REALTOR: _____   Cooperating REALTOR: _____
                                        (name of REALTOR firm)   (name of REALTOR firm)

By: _____   By: _____

Address: _____   Address: _____

_____   _____

                                                  Office ID   Office ID
Phone (Bus.)_____ (Fax)_____ Number_____   Phone (Bus.)_____ (Fax)_____ Number_____

Standard Form Copyright© 1987. Hawaii Association of REALTORS®

This form was prepared by the HAWAII ASSOCIATION OF REALTORS for use by its members.

HAWAII ASSOCIATION OF REALTORS® STANDARD FORMS

SELLER'S COUNTER OFFER 9/89

REALTOR®

REALTORS® and REALTOR-ASSOCIATES® are professionals who are members of the NATIONAL ASSOCIATION OF REALTORS® and subscribe to its strict Code of Ethics.

If this transaction involves a sale of property at a price less than $25,000, Hawaii's Plain Language Statute may apply. If so, ATTACH AN EXECUTED PLAIN LANGUAGE ADDENDUM.

Reviewed by: _____
(Principal Broker, Broker in Charge, Authorized Signature)

This is a counter offer to the attached Deposit Receipt, Offer and Acceptance ("DROA") Reference Dated _____, 19_____, submitted by (Buyer's name): _____ for the sale of the property situated at (address): _____

_____, Tax Map Key Division _____/Zone _____/Sec _____/Plat _____/Parcel _____/CPR _____.

THE BUYER'S OFFER IS NOT ACCEPTED IN ITS PRESENT FORM but this counter offer is hereby submitted **upon the same terms and conditions** set forth in said DROA including the commission agreements and Standard Terms, which are all incorporated herein by reference, with the following changes or additions to paragraphs which are checked in the box. If there are no changes in the paragraph mark N.C. in the box.

☐ 1. **PURCHASE PRICE:** _____

☐ 2. **PROPERTY DESCRIPTION:** Tax Map Key Division _____/Zone _____/Sec _____/Plat _____/Parcel _____/CPR _____

(a) **Realty:** All of that (leasehold) (fee simple) property situated at _____

_____ Hawaii, described as follows: _____

_____

(b) **Seller's Real Property Disclosure Statement** dated _____ (has) (has not) been received by Buyer. If not, address in paragraph 8, Special Terms. (b-1) **Residential Leasehold Property Addendum** (is) (is not) made a part of this DROA.

(c) **Sale Includes:** All built-in furniture, attached fixtures, built-in appliances, water heater, electrical and/or gas and plumbing fixtures, attached carpeting, existing drapes, and the following items if checked: Chandelier ( ); Range ( ); Refrigerator ( ); Disposal ( ); Dishwasher ( ); Compactor ( ); Washer ( ); Dryer ( ); Air Conditioner ( ); TV Antenna ( ); TV Cable Outlet ( ); Ceiling Fan ( ); Furnishings per attached inventory ( ); Pool Equipment ( ); and _____

_____

Specifically excluded: _____

(d) **Title:** Seller agrees to convey the property with warranties vesting marketable title in Buyer, free and clear of all liens and encumbrances except _____ and any other covenants, easements, reservations or restrictions now of record which do not materially affect the value of the property.

(e) **Assessments:** _____ shall be (paid by Seller at closing) (assumed by Buyer).

☐ 3. **FINANCING:** Buyer agrees to pay said purchase price as follows:

ADDITIONAL DEPOSIT: $ _____ in cash to be made on or before _____

$ _____ in cash at closing including all deposits herein.

$ _____ by way of _____

_____

_____

_____

$ _____ _____

$ _____ Total Purchase Price (see paragraph 1 above)

☐ 4. **CLOSING:** Closing will be on or before _____, 19_____ Escrowed by _____

☐ 5. **OCCUPANCY:** Seller agrees to give Buyer occupancy at closing or on _____, 19_____

☐ 6. **PRORATIONS:** Property taxes, lease rents, interest on assumed obligations, mortgage insurance premiums, other insurance premiums, maintenance fees, tenants' rents, if applicable, and _____ shall be prorated as of the date of closing or on _____, 19_____. Tenants' security deposit, if any, shall be charged to Seller and credited to Buyer at closing.

☐ 7. **TENANCY:** _____

☐ 8. **SPECIAL TERMS:** (Please number) _____

_____

_____

_____

_____

_____

_____

_____

_____

☐ 9. **AGENCY DISCLOSURE:** The Buyer is represented by _____ and all its salespeople. The Seller is represented by _____ and all its salespeople. Oral or written disclosure was provided before the signing of this offer.

Seller reserves the right to withdraw this counter offer at any time prior to delivery of Buyer's written acceptance to Seller's REALTOR.

EXPIRATION: This counter offer shall expire on _____, 19_____, _____ AM/PM.

_____
Name of Seller's REALTOR

by: _____

The undersigned Seller agrees to sell the above described property on the terms and conditions above set forth and acknowledges receipt of a copy of this counter offer.

_____, 19_____, _____ AM/PM.

_____
Seller's Signature

_____
Seller's Signature

_____
Name of Cooperating REALTOR

by: _____

The undersigned Buyer accepts this counter offer, agrees to buy the above described property on the terms and conditions above set forth and acknowledges receipt of a copy of this counter offer.

_____, 19_____, _____ AM/PM.

_____
Buyer's Signature

_____
Buyer's Signature

ACKNOWLEDGEMENT OF ACCEPTANCE: The undersigned acknowledges that he has been given a copy of the acceptance of this counter offer.

Date _____, 19_____, _____ AM/PM. Signature _____

GENERAL INSTRUCTIONS: This form shall be used by Seller after an initial offer has been made by the prospective buyer on a DROA form. **SELLER:** If Seller wishes to make a counter offer, Seller shall: (1) sign the DROA; (2) in paragraph 11 of the DROA, delete the words "offered above." and insert the words "per the attached Seller's Counter Offer"; and (3) indicate changes or additions on this counter offer form. **BUYER:** If Buyer wishes to make a counter offer in response to this Seller's Counter Offer, he should complete a new DROA form.

Standard Form Copyright®, 1988, Hawaii Association of REALTORS

RR204 Counter Offer

REALTORS® and REALTOR-ASSOCIATES® are professionals who are members of the NATIONAL ASSOCIATION OF REALTORS® and subscribe to its strict Code of Ethics.

STANDARD DROA ADDENDUM 1/90
The use of this form is optional.

REALTOR®

Reviewed by: _____
_____(Principal Broker, Broker in Charge, Authorized Signature)_____

This STANDARD DROA ADDENDUM is made a part of the DROA Reference Dated _____ , 19 ____ ,

by and between _____ ("Buyer")

and_____ ("Seller"),

for the sale of the property located at _____ ,

Tax Map Key No. _____ (the "Property").

THIS ADDENDUM IS DIVIDED INTO THREE SECTIONS. SECTION I INCORPORATES OTHER ADDENDA WHICH APPLY TO THE SALE OF THE PROPERTY. SECTION II CONTAINS "STANDARD TERMS" WHICH APPLY TO THE SALE OF THE PROPERTY UNLESS DELETED BY THE PARTIES. SECTION III CONTAINS "SPECIAL TERMS" WHICH WILL APPLY TO THE SALE OF THE PROPERTY ONLY IF CHECKED BY THE PARTIES. SPACE IS PROVIDED AT THE END OF SECTION III TO INCLUDE ADDITIONAL SPECIAL TERMS.

DO NOT LEAVE ANY BLANK SPACES OR EMPTY BOXES IN THIS ADDENDUM. BUYER AND SELLER AGREE THAT THE DROA IS AMENDED AS FOLLOWS:

SECTION I: INCORPORATING OTHER ADDENDA INTO THE DROA.

1.1 The following addenda (or standard forms), if checked, are attached to and made a part of this DROA.

☐ Residential Leasehold Property Addendum   ☐ Agreement to Occupy Prior to Close of Escrow

☐ Plain Language Addendum   ☐ Rental Agreement (Between Buyer and Seller)

☐ Purchase Money Mortgage Addendum   ☐ FIRPTA Affidavit

☐ Agreement of Sale Addendum   ☐ Other: _____

☐ VA Addendum   ☐ Other: _____

☐ FHA Addendum/Real Estate Certification   ☐ Other: _____

1.2 Other addenda may be identified in Paragraph 8 of this DROA. These would also be part of this DROA. Buyer and Seller should carefully read the entire DROA (including any addenda and the Standard Terms on the reverse of the DROA). All of these form a single binding contract.

SECTION II; STANDARD TERMS. Unless deleted in this DROA by Buyer and Seller, the following Standard Terms are made a part of this DROA. They may be referred to as Standard Term 1.1, Standard Term 1.2, etc.

1. REALTORS' SERVICES AND DISCLAIMERS. BUYER AND SELLER ACKNOWLEDGE THAT THEY UNDERSTAND AND AGREE TO THE FOLLOWING:

1.1 Scope Of Service. The REALTORS and any other brokers involved in this sale, including their owners, agents and employees (collectively the "REALTORS") recommend that Buyer and Seller each consult their own attorney, estate planner, CPA, accountant, design or land use professional, zoning expert, contractor, home inspector, surveyor, title insurer, termite control expert, and other professionals should they have any questions within those fields about this sale. Buyer and Seller acknowledge that they are not relying upon the REALTORS for any of the foregoing services or advice.

1.2 Disclaimers By REALTORS. The REALTORS have not made any representations or warranties, and have not rendered any opinions, about: (a) the legal or tax consequences of this transaction; or (b) the legality, validity or correctness of any building permits which may have been issued for the Property.

1.3 All Representations Are In Writing. All agreements and representations about the Property must be set forth in writing and the parties agree that any representation made by a REALTOR is set forth in writing in this DROA. Buyer and Seller shall each hold harmless and release the REALTORS from claims based upon any alleged representation which is not set forth in writing in this DROA.

2. OTHER STANDARD TERMS.

2.1 "Acceptance Date". As used in this Addendum, the term "Acceptance Date" means the date on which this contract becomes binding upon the parties (i.e. when Buyer's offer is accepted by Seller or a Seller's Counter Offer is accepted by Buyer).

2.2 (Re: Paragraph 2(b) Of The DROA) Seller's Real Property Disclosure Statement Does Not Constitute An Agreement About The Condition Of The Property. If a Seller's Real Property Disclosure Statement covering the condition of the Property is provided by Seller to Buyer, the parties understand that such Disclosure Statement contains Seller's disclosures about the existing condition of the Property. It does not constitute an agreement between the parties about the condition of the Property. Therefore, if the parties desire that certain items be sold in "AS IS" condition or that they be repaired, an appropriate Special Term must be included in this DROA.

2.3 (Re: Paragraph 2(c) Of The DROA) Title To Personal Property. All items specified in Paragraph 2(c) of this DROA shall be conveyed free and clear of any liens, mortgages and/or encumbrances, except those which Buyer may have expressly accepted or assumed as set forth elsewhere in this DROA.

2.4 Keys To The Property. At his sole cost and expense, Seller shall provide Buyer at closing or occupancy (whichever comes first): (a) any and all (but at least one set) of any entry, interior, mail box, security, and parking area keys; and (b) any garage door opener controls. Buyer agrees to pay any deposits which may be required for any of these items. Unless Buyer occupies the Property before closing, all keys and garage door opener controls will be released to Buyer only after Escrow has verbally notified Seller or Seller's REALTOR that the closing has occurred.

2.5 Home Warranty Programs. Buyer is informed that there are companies in the State of Hawaii which, for a fee, provide home warranties on appliances, improvements and other items. Buyer may purchase a home warranty, where available, at his own expense from any company Buyer chooses.

2.6 Existing Warranties (If Any), Plans, Etc. At his sole cost and expense, Seller shall provide to Buyer prior to closing: (a) all available and existing warranty documents in Seller's possession covering the improvements and personal property being sold to Buyer; and (b) all available instruction

---

BUYERS' INITIALS & DATE _____   SELLER'S INITIALS & DATE _____   Page 1 of 4

booklets in Seller's possession for appliances being sold; and (c) all available originals and copies in Seller's possession of blueprints, specifications, and architectural or engineering drawings concerning the Property. Buyer understands that: (a) any warranty documents delivered by Seller represent obligations of others, not of Seller; (b) these documents are provided for informational purposes only; and (c) Seller does not promise that any warranties are transferable to Buyer (Buyer must contact the relevant companies to determine whether the warranties are transferable to Buyer).

2.7   FIRPTA Withholding Required If Seller Is A Foreign Person. Pursuant to the Internal Revenue Code, if Seller is a foreign person or entity ("non-resident alien, corporation, etc."), Buyer must generally withhold ten percent (10%) of the "amount realized" by Seller on the sale of the Property and forward this amount to the Internal Revenue Service ("IRS"). Such withholding is not required if Buyer is purchasing the Property as a qualifying residence and the amount realized by Seller does not exceed $300,000. Unless Seller (a) provides a certification of non-foreign status to Escrow, (b) obtains a withholding exemption from the IRS, or (c) the sale otherwise is exempt from withholding, Escrow is hereby authorized and instructed (if notified in writing that withholding is required) to withhold the required amount at closing and forward it to the IRS.

2.8   FAX (Facsimile) Signatures And Counterparts. It is agreed that FAX (facsimile) copies of the executed DROA, addenda and any related documents shall be fully binding and effective for all purposes whether or not originally executed documents are transmitted to Escrow. FAX signatures on documents will be treated the same as original signatures. However, each party agrees that he will promptly forward originally executed documents to Escrow. The parties understand that they must physically execute and deliver original conveyance, mortgage and other recordable documents prior to closing. It is further agreed that this DROA, and any addenda and related documents may be executed in any number of counterparts and by different parties in separate counterparts, each of which when so signed shall be deemed to be an original, and all of which taken together shall constitute one and the same document, binding upon all of the parties, notwithstanding that all of the parties do not sign the original or the same counterparts.

2.9   (Re: Paragraph 7 Of The DROA) Tenancy. If Buyer has not yet determined the tenancy in which to purchase the Property, Buyer is advised to consult the appropriate professionals and provide Escrow with the selected tenancy by no later than thirty (30) calendar days prior to closing.

2.10   (Re: Standard Term F) Appliance Inspection. At his sole cost and expense, Buyer may have a qualified professional inspect the appliances, plumbing and electrical and/or gas fixtures described in Standard Term F on the reverse of the DROA. The REALTORS recommend such professional inspection. If Buyer does not use a qualified professional, Buyer shall not hold the REALTORS responsible for any undetected defects.

2.11   Non-Conforming Structures And Uses. Buyer is aware that some buildings are non-conforming structures or that the use of such buildings are non-conforming. This means that the structure or its use, although legal when the building was constructed or its use began, is not permitted by current zoning. This may cause some problems with respect to rebuilding, enlargement, repair, and use. It may also affect financing and resale. Buyer and Seller acknowledge that the REALTORS do not make and should not be relied upon for any determination as to non-conforming structures or uses.

2.12   Asbestos Disclosure. The United States Consumer Product Safety Commission maintains that asbestos materials are hazardous to one's health if asbestos fibers are released into the air and inhaled. Asbestos is a common insulation material on heating pipes, boilers and furnaces. It may also be present in certain types of floor and ceiling materials, shingles, plaster products, cements and other building materials. Buyer is aware that all types of structures built before 1979 (and possibly at any other time), especially those with "popcorn" or "cottage cheese" type ceilings, may contain asbestos fibers or asbestos containing material. Physically disturbing such ceilings can release asbestos fibers in the air and should only be done by licensed abatement contractors.

3.   CONTINGENCIES AND RIGHTS TO TERMINATE THIS DROA.

3.1   Contingencies. There may be contingencies stated in Section III of this Addendum or elsewhere in this DROA. A contingency means that the obligation of Buyer to buy or Seller to sell the Property is conditioned upon the timely occurrence of certain event(s). If any contingency is not satisfied within the specified time limit, then the party designated in the contingency may elect to: (a) terminate this DROA by giving Escrow written notice with copies to all parties to this contract by no later than five (5) calendar days following the expiration of the time limit; or (b) waive the contingency. If timely written notice to terminate is given, the provisions of Standard Term 3.2 shall apply. If timely written notice to terminate is not given, then the contingency shall be deemed to be waived, the party designated in the contingency shall be deemed to have waived his right to terminate this DROA on account of such contingency, and the parties will remain bound under this DROA.

3.2   Termination Provision. If Buyer or Seller elects to terminate this DROA pursuant to Standard Term 3.1, then: (a) each of the parties agree to promptly execute the cancellation documents requested by Escrow; and (b) Escrow shall return to Buyer all deposits previously made, less the amount of any escrow expenses or fees chargeable to Buyer. Thereafter, neither Buyer, Seller, Escrow, nor any REALTORS shall have any further rights or obligations under this DROA.

SECTION III: SPECIAL TERMS. Place a check-mark in a box to make the appropriate Special Term a part of this DROA. A Special Term may be referred to as Special Term 1.1, Special Term 1.2, etc. State "N/A" in the box if the Special Term is not a part of this DROA. Do not leave any empty boxes.

1.   DEPOSITS AND CASH FUNDS.

1.1   Initial Deposit. Buyer's initial deposit check remains uncashed. It will be retained by the REALTOR assisting Buyer and will be deposited with Escrow shortly after the Acceptance Date.

1.2   Interest On Deposits.

1.2.1.   Buyer To Earn Interest. The parties instruct Escrow to place Buyer's initial and additional deposits, if any, in an interest bearing account with all interest to accrue and be credited to Buyer at closing. Buyer will pay any processing fee required by Escrow, and all costs of setting up, maintaining and closing the account. Buyer's Social Security Number or Federal Identification Number is:

_____ . Buyer understands that such fees and costs may exceed the interest earned.

1.2.2   Buyer Not To Earn Interest. Buyer hereby waives the right to place Buyer's deposits in an interest bearing account. Buyer understands that unless Escrow is instructed to open such an account in Special Term 1.2.1, all interest earned on any deposits will accrue to the benefit of Escrow.

1.3   No Contingency On Obtaining "Cash Funds". Buyer represents that there are no contingencies to Buyer's obtaining the down payment and cash portion of the purchase price and closing costs to buy the Property (collectively the "Cash Funds"). Buyer (a) shall not delay (or extend) closing to obtain the Cash Funds, and (b) shall deliver to Escrow prior to the scheduled closing date cash, or a cashier's or certified check for the Cash Funds from a local financial institution made payable to Escrow, or properly wired funds.

1.4   Buyer's Contingency On Obtaining Cash Funds. There are contingencies to Buyer obtaining the Cash Funds. The contingencies are as follows:_____
_____
_____ .

If Buyer does not obtain the Cash Funds by the closing date, Buyer may terminate this DROA pursuant to Standard Term 3.1.

2.   FINANCING ISSUES.

2.1   Financing Contingency. The obligation of Buyer to purchase the Property is conditioned upon Buyer obtaining the financing described in this DROA ("Buyer's Mortgage Loan") by the closing date. If Buyer does not obtain Buyer's Mortgage Loan, Buyer may terminate this DROA pursuant to Standard Term 3.1.

Buyer may increase Buyer's portion of Cash Funds at closing and thereby reduce the amount of Buyer's Mortgage Loan. Buyer may also waive this financing contingency and proceed with this transaction on an all cash basis. If Buyer elects either of these two options, Buyer shall promptly give written notice of such election to Escrow and to Seller.

BUYERS' INITIALS & DATE _____   SELLER'S INITIALS & DATE _____   Page 2 of 4

☐ 2.2 Buyer's Mortgage Loan.

2.2.1 Buyer's Agreements Relating To Buyer's Mortgage Loan. Buyer shall use his best efforts to obtain Buyer's Mortgage Loan, which shall include such things as doing the following: (1) submitting a complete loan application package (including the payment of fees for a credit report and appraisal) by no later than _____ ( ) calendar days after the Acceptance Date; (2) delivering to Seller a loan prequalification letter from the lender or providing the lender's verbal loan approval by no later than _____ ( ) calendar days after the loan application package is submitted (such verbal approval to consist of lender stating that — on review of Buyer's loan application documents and subject only to verification of items therein, the credit report(s), and appraisal — Buyer should be qualified for, and lender should be able to make the loan); and (3) delivering to Seller a loan commitment letter by no later than _____ ( ) calendar days after the Acceptance Date.

2.2.2 Seller's Right To Terminate DROA. Seller's obligation to sell the Property is conditioned upon Buyer meeting each of the deadlines specified in Special Term 2.2.1. If any deadline is not met, Seller may terminate this DROA pursuant to Standard Term 3.1. However, this Special Term 2.2.2 shall no longer apply if Buyer has given written notice of Buyer's election to proceed with this transaction on an all cash basis pursuant to Special Term 2.1.

2.2.3 Buyer's Agreements Relating To Providing And Authorizing Disclosure Of Information. Buyer shall provide Seller's REALTOR and Escrow the name of the lender and the loan officer within _____ ( ) calendar days after the Acceptance Date. Buyer hereby authorizes Seller and Seller's REALTOR to contact Buyer's lender and Escrow regarding the status of Buyer's loan application.

3. PROPERTY CONDITION ISSUES.

3.1 (Re: Paragraph 2(b) Of The DROA And Standard Term 2.2.) Seller's Real Property Disclosure Statement.

☐ 3.1.1 Receipt And Approval Of Disclosure Statement. Buyer acknowledges (a) receipt of the Hawaii Association of REALTORS Seller's Real Property Disclosure Statement ("Disclosure Statement") dated _____ , 19_____ and (b) his approval of it.

☐ 3.1.2 Disclosure Statement To Be Provided. Seller shall complete and deliver to Buyer the Disclosure Statement for the Property within _____ ( ) calendar days after the Acceptance Date. The information contained in the Disclosure Statement shall be current as of the date it is provided to Buyer.

☐ 3.1.3 Contingency On Timely Delivery Of Disclosure Statement. The obligation of Buyer to purchase the Property is conditioned upon Seller's delivery of the completed Disclosure Statement to Buyer within the time limit specified in Special Term 3.1.2. If Seller does not deliver the completed Disclosure Statement within such time limit, Buyer may terminate this DROA pursuant to Standard Term 3.1.

☐ 3.1.4 Contingency On Buyer's Approval Of Disclosure Statement. The obligation of Buyer to purchase the Property is conditioned upon Buyer's approval of the Disclosure Statement within _____ ( ) calendar days of receipt from Seller. If Buyer disapproves of the Disclosure Statement, Buyer may terminate this DROA pursuant to Standard Term 3.1.

☐ 3.1.5 Updates To Disclosure Statement. Seller shall promptly update the Disclosure Statement if Seller discovers any materially adverse fact prior to closing, which would affect the accuracy or completeness of the Disclosure Statement. If the Disclosure Statement is updated, then the obligation of Buyer to purchase the Property is conditioned upon Buyer's approval of the updated Disclosure Statement within _____ ( ) calendar days of Buyer's receipt from Seller. If Buyer disapproves of the Disclosure Statement, Buyer may terminate this DROA pursuant to Standard Term 3.1. This Special Term 3.1.5 shall apply to each update to the Disclosure Statement if there is more than one. This right to terminate does not require Buyer to terminate this DROA or limit Buyer's rights or remedies, if any, in the event Buyer decides to proceed with this DROA despite the updated Disclosure Statement.

☐ 3.2 Inspection Of Property By Experts Of Buyer's Choice. Buyer, at his sole cost and expense: (a) may obtain an inspection of all or any part of the Property by any expert, professional, or other representative of Buyer's choice; and (b) may inspect the Property and any public records relating to the Property. The REALTOR assisting Buyer may also inspect the Property and any public records. Seller shall give Buyer and Buyer's representatives access to the Property to enable such inspections to be carried out. Such inspections shall be made during reasonable hours with reasonable prior notice to Seller.

The obligation of Buyer to purchase the Property is conditioned upon Buyers's approval of the results of any inspection performed pursuant to the preceding paragraph, within _____ ( ) calendar days after the Acceptance Date. Any inspections must be completed within this time period. If Buyer does not approve of said results within such time period, Buyer may terminate this DROA pursuant to Standard Term 3.1. For purposes of this Special Term 3.2, Buyer shall be deemed to have approved any material defect or damage which had previously been: (a) disclosed in writing by Seller to Buyer (in the Seller's Real Property Disclosure Statement or otherwise), and (b) accepted by Buyer.

☐ 3.2.1 Seller's Election To Repair. If any inspection reveals previously undisclosed material defects or damage, then Seller may elect to repair, at his sole cost and expense, all such defects or damage, prior to closing. If Seller so elects, Buyer may not terminate this DROA pursuant to Special Term 3.2 or Standard Term 3.1. Any such repair shall be made by a licensed contractor acceptable to Buyer. If Seller elects to make such repairs, then the obligation of Buyer to purchase the Property is conditioned upon Seller completing and paying for such repairs prior to closing. However, Seller may unilaterally extend the closing date for a reasonable time to complete such repairs. If Seller does not complete the repairs, Buyer may terminate this DROA pursuant to Standard Term 3.1.

☐ 3.3 (Re: Standard Term E) Termite Report And Substantial Termite Damage. The obligation of Buyer to purchase the Property is conditioned upon Buyer's review and approval of the termite report obtained by Seller pursuant to Standard Term E, within _____ ( ) calendar days of receipt from Seller. If Buyer does not approve of said report within such time period, Buyer may terminate this DROA pursuant to Standard Term 3.1. For purposes of this Special Term, Buyer shall be deemed to have approved of: any termite report which does not reveal substantial termite damage; or any termite report which does reveal substantial termite damage which had previously been: (a) disclosed in writing by Seller to Buyer (in the Seller's Real Property Disclosure Statement or otherwise); and (b) accepted by Buyer.

☐ 3.3.1 Seller's Election To Repair. If the termite report reveals previously undisclosed substantial termite damage, Seller may elect to repair, at his sole cost and expense, all such damage, prior to closing. If Seller so elects, then Buyer may not terminate this DROA pursuant to Special Term 3.3 or Standard Term 3.1. Any such repair shall be made by a licensed contractor acceptable to Buyer. If Seller elects to make such repairs, then the obligation of Buyer to purchase the Property is conditioned upon Seller completing and paying for such repairs prior to closing. However, Seller may unilaterally extend the closing date for a reasonable time to complete such repairs. If Seller does not complete the repairs, Buyer may terminate this DROA pursuant to Standard Term 3.1.

4. PROPERTY CONDITION ISSUES — BUYER'S AND SELLER'S AGREEMENTS.

☐ 4.1 (Re: Property Condition) Interior Cleaning. At his sole cost and expense, prior to closing, Seller shall have professionally cleaned the interior of the improvements on the Property and all appliances. Such cleaning shall include all appliances, floors, carpets, windows, jalousies, and screens.

BUYERS' INITIALS & DATE _____   SELLER'S INITIALS & DATE _____   Page 3 of 4

4.2 Pet Related Carpet Treatment And Fumigation. At his sole cost and expense, prior to closing, Seller shall have any pets removed, the carpets within the improvements on the Property professionally cleaned, and the interior of the Property treated for fleas/ticks by a professional exterminator. There shall be a follow-up fumigation/egg hatch treatment which may take place prior to or within two (2) weeks after closing or occupancy (whichever comes first).

4.3 (Re: Property Condition) Maintenance. Seller agrees that at closing or occupancy (whichever comes first), the air conditioning (if any), electrical, lighting (including light bulbs), sewer, drainage, lawn sprinkler system (if any), and plumbing systems (including solar water heater, if applicable), major appliances, mechanical devices (including all locks and window hardware) and screens shall be in working order and good repair. If such conditions exist, Seller shall replace, prior to closing, any cracked or broken glass (including windows, mirrors, shower and tub enclosures) and any torn or separated screens. Seller shall maintain (in the same condition and repair as they were in on the Acceptance Date) the interior and exterior of the Property, existing landscaping, grounds, lawn, and any pool, until closing (or occupancy, whichever comes first). All of the foregoing shall be at Seller's sole cost and expense.

4.4 (Re: Standard Term C) — Survey. Delete Standard Term C on the reverse of the DROA. At his sole cost and expense, prior to closing, Seller shall, even if pins are visible, have a licensed surveyor stake the Property and provide to Buyer a sketch showing any encroachments. If any encroachments are found, then Buyer may terminate this DROA pursuant to Standard Term 3.1.

4.5 (Re: Standard Term F) Walk-Through And Appliance Check. Buyer shall complete his inspection in accordance with Standard Term F by no later than _____ ( ) calendar days prior to closing or occupancy (whichever comes first). Seller shall comply with the provisions of Standard Term F. Should there be any malfunction of items covered by Standard Term F between the inspection and closing, Seller shall make repairs to return these items to working order consistent with their age.

Should the Seller be unable to make the repairs required by Standard Term F and/or this Special Term 4.5 by closing, Seller agrees that an amount equal to 150% of the estimated cost of repair shall be withheld in Escrow until the repairs are completed; provided, however, that any and all remaining funds will be automatically disbursed to Buyer by Escrow if all repairs are not completed within three (3) weeks after closing. All repair bills will be paid through Escrow and any balance remaining upon completion of repairs (prior to three (3) weeks after closing) shall be returned to Seller. Seller will order any repairs required pursuant to this Special Term 4.5 prior to closing. Buyer will order any repairs required pursuant to this Special Term 4.5 after closing.

5. GENERAL ISSUES.

5.1 Community Association Dues. Buyer is aware that the Property is located in an area or neighborhood which assesses fees for _____.

The fees are currently $ _____ per month and may increase in the future.

5.2 Rental Property. If the Property is rented, Buyer understands that Seller and the REALTORS are not offering to sell or selling the Property together with any existing or future rental pool or other rental arrangements. Seller and the REALTORS make no representations or guarantees about future rents or future resale value. Buyer understands that he is assuming all risks relating to the foregoing, including the rental of the Property, should Buyer wish to rent it out.

5.3 Mediation And Arbitration. If any dispute or claim in law or equity arises out of this DROA, Buyer and Seller agree in good faith to attempt to settle such dispute or claim by mediation under the Commercial Mediation rules of the American Arbitration Association. If such mediation is not successful in resolving such dispute or claim, then such dispute or claim shall be decided by neutral binding arbitration before a single arbitrator in accordance with the Commercial Arbitration rules of the American Arbitration Association. Judgment upon the award rendered by the arbitrator may be entered in any court having jurisdiction thereof.

Any dispute or claim by or against any REALTOR and/or real estate licensee participating in this sale shall be submitted to mediation followed by binding arbitration consistent with the above provisions.

5.4 Disclosure Of Real Estate Licensing Status. Real estate licensees in the State of Hawaii are required to disclose that they hold a real estate license in any transaction in which they are purchasing or selling real property as a principal, or representing a relative or an entity in which they have any interest. If applicable, the licensees in this transaction shall disclose their licensing status in the space provided below.

_____
_____
_____

6. ADDITIONAL SPECIAL TERMS. Please Number 6.1, 6.2, etc.

_____
_____
_____
_____
_____
_____
_____
_____
_____
_____
_____
_____
_____
_____

The undersigned acknowledge that they have read, understood and agreed to the terms and conditions of this Standard DROA Addendum, and further acknowledge receipt of a completed copy hereof.

BUYER _____   SELLER _____

BUYER _____   SELLER _____

DATE _____ TIME _____ AM/PM   DATE _____ TIME _____ AM/PM

SELLER'S REAL PROPERTY DISCLOSURE STATEMENT
Single-Family Residences and Vacant Land

PROPERTY ADDRESS _____

SELLER'S NAME _____

Single-Family Residence _____ Vacant Land _____

TO THE BEST OF MY KNOWLEDGE, WHICH IS THAT OF A LAYMAN AND NOT OF AN EXPERT, THE CONDITION OF THIS PROPERTY IS AS INDICATED BELOW:

1. BUILDINGS AND OTHER IMPROVEMENTS

a. What is the approximate age of the home? _____ Do you have the house plans? _____ Will they be transferred to the buyer? _____
Who were the architect and builder? _____

b. What is the age of the roof of the main building and all other buildings? _____
Is there a continuing warranty in effect? _____ If so, give name and address of warrantor and length of time remaining _____
_____

c. Does any part of the building or buildings leak? _____ If so, please explain in full _____
_____
Have you ever had any leaks repaired? _____ If so, please explain, and state by whom and whether a continuing warranty is in effect _____
_____

d. Has there been prior termite and/or dry rot damage? _____ If so, please explain _____
_____

e. Have there been any additions and/or structural changes or remodeling, including, but not limited to, electrical and plumbing work? _____ If so,
please explain, and state by whom the work was done and whether continuing warranties are available _____
_____
Were all necessary permits obtained? _____ If not, please explain _____
_____

f. Have there been any problems involving the foundation, lawn or plants, sprinklers, walls, fences, pool or equipment? _____ If so, please
explain _____
_____ Are any plants to be removed? _____

g. Does the main house have gutters on all sides? _____ What type? _____ Condition? _____

h. Are all the built-ins and appliances to be included in the sale owned by Seller? _____ If not, who is the owner and will the built-ins remain?
_____

2. LAND

a. Does the property have any filled ground? _____ If so, is the house built on filled or unstable ground? _____

b. Is there any known slippage in the neighborhood? _____ If so, please explain _____
_____

c. Do you know of any past or present settling or soil movement problems on the property or on adjacent properties? _____ If so, have they resulted
in any structural damage? _____ What was the extent of the damage? _____
_____ If so, was it repaired? _____

d. Do you know of any past or present drainage problem on your property or adjacent properties? _____ Does water ever stand on the property?
_____ If so, please explain _____
_____

3. Are there any known toxic substances in the soil, the water supply, or the air? _____ If so, please explain _____
_____

f. Are you aware of any encroachments on the boundaries of this property? _____ If so, please explain _____
_____
Are all survey pins visible? _____ Who owns the walls and fences on the property? _____
Are you aware of any encroachments onto any adjoining property _____ If so, please explain _____
_____

g. What is the current zoning of the property? _____ Have you applied for a change of zoning? _____ When? _____ What is the status of
the application? _____

h. What is the flood zone or tsunami zone classification? _____ Is flood insurance required? _____ Are building or rebuilding restrictions in
effect as a result of the hazard designation? _____ If so, please explain _____
_____

i. Has earthquake damage occurred to this property or in the neighborhood? _____ Was it repaired? _____ Please explain _____

j. Is this property in a volcano hazard area? _____ If so, is insurance available? _____ Any insurance restrictions? _____

3. UTILITIES

a. Is the property legally connected to the public sewer line? _____ If not, please explain _____
If property is on cesspool, septic tank or other sanitation system, where is it located? _____

b. Are any utility assessments (sewer, street lighting, other) existing or contemplated? _____ If so, please explain _____
_____

c. What type of plumbing pipe material is used in this property? _____
Describe any pipe replacement _____

d. Have there been any problems with the plumbing (including solar system, septic tank, or other), electrical, water and/or gas? _____ If so,
please explain _____
_____

e. What is the size of the water heater? _____ When was it installed? _____ Solar system? _____ When installed? _____ How
many panels? _____ Continuing Warranty? _____ From whom? _____

f. What is the source of the water supply? _____ If catchment, what is the cistern or tank size? _____ Age? _____ Construction?
_____ Type of pump? _____ Any leaks? _____ If so, please explain _____
_____

g. What is the approximate age of the electrical system? _____ Type of wiring? _____ Multibreaker? _____ Fuse system? _____
New wiring? _____ Any problems with the wiring? _____ If so, please explain _____
_____
Outdoor wiring? _____ Existing 220V service? _____

h. If the property has an alternative power system, is there a generator? _____ Type? _____ Capacity? _____ Age? _____
Photovoltaic? _____ Output? _____ Age? _____

	Buyer's Initials	Seller's Initials
	_____/_____	_____/_____

RR102

4. TITLE

a. Do you have a clear legal title to this property? _____

b. Do you own real property adjacent to, across the street from, or in the same subdivision as this property? _____ If so, please explain _____

c. Is the property part of a mandatory community association? _____ Will association documents be provided to buyers? _____

d. Is an interest in such common elements as roads, parks or common areas, or recreational facilities included with this property? _____ If so, please explain _____

e. Is the property currently under lease to a tenant? _____ Expiration date? _____ Does the tenant have an option to extend the lease? If so, until when? _____

f. Do you know of easements, licenses, restrictive covenants, boundary disputes, or third-party claims affecting this property (rights of other people to interfere with the use of this property or adjoining property in any way? _____ If so, please explain _____

g. Is there any litigation, existing or contemplated, involving this property, or against its owners or developers? _____ If so, please explain _____

h. Are there any delinquent taxes (income, real property, business-related, or other) that might involve this property? _____ If so, please explain

i. If property is leasehold:

Has fee purchase been voluntarily offered? _____ What are its terms and deadlines? _____

Has a condemnation suit been filed? _____ When? _____ Are you a part of the suit? _____ How much deposit have you paid and when? _____ How much deposit is owed and when? _____

Number and status of the suit? _____

Is there a court date? _____ Which is the law firm representing the owners in the condemnation suit? _____

From whom may a buyer obtain further information? _____

5. PENDING CHANGES

a. Do you know of any action, passed or contemplated (road widening, zoning change, rights of way, or other), that might affect this property? _____ If so, please explain _____

b. Are you aware of any pending real estate development in this area (condominiums, cluster or planned unit developments, subdivisions or commercial, education religious, industrial uses, for example)? _____ If so, please explain _____

6. QUIET ENJOYMENT

a. Do you experience any excessive noise at this property (airplanes, animals, traffic, neighbors, schools)? _____ If so, please explain _____

b. Is there any industry or operation in your community which is considered to be controversial and/or possibly dangerous? _____ If so, please explain _____

c. Are you aware of any notorious incidents in the social history of this property? _____ If so, please explain _____

7. NEWLY CONSTRUCTED RESIDENCES OR ADDITIONS

a. Has the property or addition received a Certificate of Completion? _____ When was Public Notice filed? _____ What material, labor and/or builder continuing warranties exist? _____ Will copies of continuing warranties be provided to buyer? _____

b. If property is incomplete:

Is there a completion bond? _____ What amount? _____ Issued by? _____ Held by? _____ Copy available for buyer? _____ Are funds for completion held in a trust fund? _____ Where? _____ Who may authorize their release? _____

Is there construction insurance on the uncompleted property? _____ Issued by? _____ Copy available for buyer? _____

c. Who are the developers of the property? _____

Contractor? _____ Subcontractors? _____

Investors? _____ Architect? _____

Development Lender? _____

d. Are the builders and developers of the property members of the Homebuilders Association, Building Industry Association, or any other professional building association? _____ Name _____

PLEASE MAKE FURTHER EXPLANATIONS OR ADD ANY OTHER INFORMATION HERE _____

8. REVERSIONARY OR SURRENDER CLAUSE

Is there a reversionary or surrender clause in the lease? _____ If so, please explain _____

9. DISCLOSURE

My broker, _____ has advised me that it is advisable to make known any fact, defect or condition, past or present, relating to my property that a buyer might want and/or need to know. Other than listed above, there are no facts, defects or conditions known to me.

THIS STATEMENT IS A DISCLOSURE OF THE CONDITION OF THE PROPERTY BASED ON MY LAYMAN'S OBSERVATION OF VISIBLE, ACCESSIBLE AREAS, DOCUMENTS, AND CONDITIONS AND IS NOT A WARRANTY OF ANY KIND BY MYSELF OR MY AGENT AND IS NOT A SUBSTITUTE FOR ANY EXPERT INSPECTIONS OR WARRANTIES THAT THE BUYER MAY WISH TO OBTAIN.

I have received a copy of this completed Seller's Real Property Disclosure Statement, which includes _____ pages or the reverse of this sheet. I am aware this information may be made available to prospective buyers.

_____   _____
Signature of Owner   Signature of Owner

_____   _____
Date   Date

_____
Signature of Other Owners and Dates

SELLER'S REAL PROPERTY DISCLOSURE STATEMENT
Condominium Apartment and Townhouse

REALTOR®

PROPERTY ADDRESS AND UNIT NUMBER _____

SELLER'S NAME _____

TO THE BEST OF MY KNOWLEDGE, WHICH IS THAT OF A LAYMAN AND NOT OF AN EXPERT, THE CONDITION OF THIS PROPERTY IS AS INDICATED BELOW:

1. **BUILDING**
   a. Current Name of Building _____
   Previous Name of Building _____
   b. Tax Map Key _____ HPR _____ Public Report # _____
   c. Age of Building _____ years
   Number of Units in Building _____ Number of Floors _____ Number of Elevators _____
   Construction: Interior Walls _____ Exterior Walls _____

2. **MANAGEMENT**
   a. Name and Address of Management Company _____
   b. Name of Account Executive _____ Telephone Number _____
   c. Resident Manager: Name and Phone Number _____
   d. President of Homeowners' Association _____
   e. Please check availability of copies of the following documents:
   Condominium Declaration and Amendments _____ Current House Rules _____ Homeowners' Association Bylaws and Amendments
   Ground Lease _____ Current Association Budget and Financial Statements _____
   f. What is the current maintenance fee for this unit? _____ When was it last changed? _____ What does it include? _____
   Back fees owed? _____ Paid by whom and when? _____
   g. Has your Association notified you of future maintenance-fee increases or special assessments? _____ If so, please explain _____
   _____
   h. Please name the insurer for the building or project (master Homeowners' Association policy) _____
   includes _____ Is flood insurance needed and/or carried by the Association? _____
   If so, name the insurer _____
   i. Have there been any problems (water, settling, vibration or other) in this unit or any unit or common element in the building? _____ If so, please explain _____
   j. Do you know of any pending or existing lawsuits against this building or by the Association or involving this unit? _____ If so, please explain _____
   _____
   Circuit Court Number _____ Copy Available? _____
   k. Are there any special assessments in effect? _____ If so, what type of assessment (legal, repair, City & County, etc.) _____
   Total amount for this unit? $_____ For the building? $_____ When are payments due? _____ Amount per payment?
   $_____ Back payments to be satisfied? _____ By whom? _____

3. **RESTRICTIONS**
   a. Are children allowed in this building? _____ Ages? _____
   b. Number of occupants allowed for this unit? _____
   c. Are pets allowed? _____ Number per unit? _____ Kind of pets? _____
   d. Any restrictions on rentals in this building? _____
   e. Do you need approval for exterior or interior alterations? _____
   f. Are there any restrictions on resale of units in the building or of this unit? _____ If so, please explain _____

4. **PARKING**
   a. How many parking stalls are included in the sale of this unit? _____ How many covered? _____ Standard _____ Compact _____
   Tandem _____ Number or letters _____
   b. Is there guest parking available for the building? _____ Where? _____ How many stalls? _____

5. **STORAGE**
   a. Are there any storage spaces that are included in the purchase of this unit? _____ How many? _____ Where are they? _____
   Numbers or letters: _____ Approximate size _____
   b. Are the storage spaces individual or a common room? _____

6. **COMMERCIAL OR RESORT USE**
   a. Are there any commercial, timeshare, or resort uses existing or pending in this building or project? _____ Is it year-round? _____
   b. Have there been any problems with these usages? _____ If so, please explain _____
   c. Do these units pay extra maintenance or management fees? _____

7. **SECURITY**
   a. What are the security arrangements for this building? _____
   b. Which and how many of these security items will be provided to the new Owners? _____ Building Security Keys _____ Parking
   entry devices _____ Mail box keys _____ Unit keys, including deadbolt _____ Storage keys _____ Other necessary access
   and security items _____

8. **FEES AND DEPOSITS**
   a. Which of these fees and deposits are required? (Please state amount, refundability, recipient and who will pay).
   Transfer fee _____
   Registration fees _____
   Move-in fees _____
   Security devices (keys, cards, genies) _____
   Pet deposit fees _____
   Other _____

9. **APPLIANCES**
   a. Are all the appliances, mechanical equipment, accessories, and built-ins presently situated in the unit and to be included in the sale in good condition and satisfactory working order? _____ If not, please explain what and who will repair _____

Buyer's Initials	Seller's Initials
_____/_____	_____/_____

RR105

10. PLUMBING AND ELECTRICAL

a. Have you had any problems with the plumbing or electrical fixtures or systems? _____ If so, please explain _____

_____

b. Where are the circuit breakers? _____

c. Is access for cable-TV installation available in this building? _____

d. Are phone jacks available in this building and unit? _____

e. Does any part of the building or buildings leak? _____ If so, please explain in full _____

_____

Have you ever had any leaks repaired? _____ If so, please explain, and state by whom and whether a continuing warranty is in effect _____

_____

f. Has there been prior termite and/or dry rot damage? _____ If so, please explain _____

_____

11. FLOOR COVERINGS

a. What are the types and approximate ages of the floor coverings? _____

_____

b. General condition? _____

c. Are there any differences in color or condition currently not visible? _____ If so, please explain _____

_____

12. ADDITIONS, REPAIRS, SPECIAL FEATURES

a. Item, cost, date, and who performed work

_____

_____

_____

b. Was permission needed and obtained from the Association or lessor or anyone else? _____ If so, please explain _____

c. Are warranties available and from whom? _____

13. PENDING CHANGES

a. Do you know of any action, passed or contemplated (road widening, zoning change, rights of way or other) that might affect this property? _____ If so, please explain _____

_____

b. Are you aware of any pending real estate development in this area (condominiums, cluster or planned unit developments, subdivisions or commercial, education, religious, industrial uses, for example)? _____

_____ If so, please explain _____

14. QUIET ENJOYMENT

a. Do you experience any excessive noise at this property (airplanes, animals, traffic, neighbors, schools)? _____ If so, please explain _____

_____

b. Is there any industry or operation in your community which is considered to be controversial and/or possibly dangerous? _____ If so, please explain _____

c. Are you aware of any notorious incidents in the social history of this property? _____ If so, please explain _____

_____

15. TITLE

a. Do you have clear legal title to this property? _____

b. Name all owners of this property other than the persons signing below _____ _____

_____

c. Does anyone have a right of first refusal, option, life interest or lease in or on this property? _____ If so, please explain _____

d. Are there any liens or judgements against this property or its owners? _____ If so, please explain in full _____

e. Are there any delinquent taxes (income, property, busienss-related) that might affect this property? _____ If so, please explain _____

f. If the property is leasehold:

Has fee purchase been voluntarily offered? _____ What are its terms and deadlines? _____

Has a condemnation suit been filed? _____ When? _____ Are you a part of the suit? _____ How much deposit have you paid and when? _____ How much deposit is owed and when? _____ Number and status of the suit? _____

Is there a court date? _____ Which is the law firm representing the owners in the condemnation suit? _____ From whom may a buyer obtain further information? _____

g. What is the current zoning of this property? _____ Could the same number and size of units be rebuilt if the building were destroyed by fire or natural causes? _____ If so, please explain _____

h. Is there action, contemplated or in effect (road widening, rights of way, zoning or other), that will affect this property? _____ If not, please explain _____

_____

PLEASE MAKE FURTHER EXPLANATIONS OR ADD ANY OTHER INFORMATION HERE _____

_____

_____

_____

16. REVERSIONARY OR SURRENDER CLAUSE

Is there a reversionary or surrender clause in the lease? _____ If so, please explain _____

17. DISCLOSURE

My broker, _____, has advised me that it is advisable to make known any fact, defect or condition, past or present relating to my property that a buyer might want and/or need to know. Other than listed above, there are no facts, defects or conditions known to me.

THIS STATEMENT IS A DISCLOSURE OF THE CONDITION OF THE PROPERTY BASED ON MY LAYMAN'S OBSERVATION OF VISIBLE, ACCESSIBLE AREAS, DOCUMENTS, AND CONDITIONS AND IS NOT A WARRANTY OF ANY KIND BY MYSELF OR MY AGENT AND IS NOT A SUBSTITUTE FOR ANY EXPERT INSPECTIONS OR WARRANTIES THAT THE BUYER MAY WISH TO OBTAIN.

I have received a copy of this completed Seller's Real Property Disclosure Statement, which includes _____ pages or the reverse side of this sheet. I am aware this information may be made available to prospective buyers.

_____

Signature of Owner

_____

Date

_____

Signature of Owner

_____

Date

_____

Signature of Other Owners and Dates

Cases and Statutes Cited

1. *Pae v. Stevens,* 256 F.2d 208 (Hawaii 1958).
2. Section 560:5-101, *Hawaii Revised Statutes.*
3. Sections 501-101.5(c) and 502-85, *Hawaii Revised Statutes.*
4. *Jenkins v. Wise,* 58 Haw. 592, 574 P.2d 1337 (1978).
5. Employee Retirement Income Security Act of 1974.
6. *Clark v. Title Guaranty Co., Etc.,* 44 Haw. 261, 265, 353 P.2d 1002 (1960).
7. *Kipahulu Investment Co. v. Seltzer Partnership,* 4 Haw. App. 625, 675 P.2d 778 (1983).
8. *Clark v. Title Guaranty Co., Etc.,* 44 Haw. 261, 265, 353 P.2d 1002 (1960).
9. *In Re Application of Ashford,* 50 Haw. 314, 315, 440 P.2d 76 (1968).
10. *County of Hawaii v. Sotomura,* 55 Haw. 176, 182, 517 P.2d 57 (1973).
11. *Sotomura v. County of Hawaii,* 460 F. Supp. 473, 478, 480 (1978).
12. Act 188, Session Laws of Hawaii (1977).
13. *Sawada v. Endo,* 57 Haw. 608, 561 P.2d 1291 (1977).
14. *Burgess v. Arita,* 5 Haw. App. 581, 704 P.2d 930 (1985).
15. *Village of Euclid v. Ambler Realty Co.,* 272 U.S. 365, 47 Sup.Ct. 114, 71 L.Ed. 303 (1926).
16. Act 307, Session Laws of Hawaii 1967.
17. *Jones v. Alfred Mayer Co.,* 392 U.S. 409, 88 Sup.Ct. 2186, 20 L.E.2d 1189 (1968).
18. Article I, Section 20, *Hawaii Constitution.*
19. Article II, Part I, Uniform Probate Code, Chapter 560, Hawaii Revised Statutes.
20. Chapter 560, *Hawaii Revised Statutes.*

Index

abstract, 75–76
acceleration clause, 63
acknowledgment, 94, 111
agent, definition of, 23
agreement of sale, 69–71
annual percentage rate (APR), 68
AOAO (association of apartment owners), 9
appraisal, definition of, 31
assessment, 120
association of apartment owners (AOAO), 9
attorney-in-fact, 52

bill of sale, 6

CAP (Consolidated Application Process), 91
capitalize, 35
Civil Rights Act of 1866, 142
Coastal Zone Management Program, 90
common elements, 10
comparables, 20, 32
competence, 42–44
condominium, 9–12
Consolidated Application Process (CAP), 91
contract, voidable, 43
cooperative apartments (co-op), 12–14
corporation, 45–46
Corps of Engineers, 90
chattels, 5
closing date, 93
closing statement, 97
collateral, 62
cost approach to appraisal, 33–34

Declaration of Covenants, Conditions, and Restrictions, 15
deed, 5
discount points, 65–66
due on sale clause, 64

easement, 79–81
elective share, 153
eminent domain, 144
encumbrance, 76
escheat, 153
estate at will, 161–162
estate for years, 161–162

Fair Housing Act of 1968, 142–143
fair market value, definition of, 32

fee simple, 8, 160
fiduciary, 23–24
File Plan Map, 78–79
fixtures, definition of, 6
foreclosures, 64, 147–150
freehold estates, 159

grace period, 63
guardianship, 50–52

Hawaii Housing Authority, 140
Hawaii Land Reform Act, 139–141
holdover tenant, 162
homeowners associations, 16
homeowner's insurance policy, 136

income approach to appraisal, 34–36
institutional properties, 18
intestacy law, 152

land, definition of, 4
Land Court, 112–115
leasehold estates, 139, 159–162
legal description, 76–77
lien, 81–82
life estate, 160
limited common elements, 10, 11
liquidated damage, definition of, 126
lis pendens, 83
listing: definition of, 27; types of, 27–30
loan points, 65
loan-to-value ratio, 66

market approach to appraisal, 32
marketable title, 75
metes and bounds, 77
mortgage, 62–69

National Flood Insurance Program, 136

ohana housing, 9
origination points, 65

partnership, 46–48
periodic estate, 161–162
personal property, definition of, 5
personalty, definition of, 5
power of attorney, definition of, 52

principal, 23, 52
probate, 102, 152
promissory note, 62–63
proprietary lease, 12
proration, 96–97
protected person, definition of, 50
purchase money mortgage, 69

real estate, definition of, 4
real estate recovery fund, 25
Real Estate Settlement Procedures Act
    (RESPA), 97
real property, definition of, 5
realtor, 20
realty, definition of, 4
release of mortgage, 64
remainderman, 160
replacement cost, definition of, 34
reproduction cost, definition of, 34
Residential Landlord-Tenant Code, 141–
    142
RESPA (Real Estate Settlement Procedures
    Act), 97

restrictive covenant, 15
reversion, 160–161

shoreline setback, 87–90
Statute of Frauds, 55–56
subdivision, definition of, 14–16

tenancy: in common, 105–106; by the
    entirety, 102–104; joint, 104–105; in
    severalty, 101–102
tenancy at sufferance, 161–162
time sharing, 16–18
title, definition of, 75
title report, 76
Torrens system, 113
transfer certificate of title, 114
trust, 48–50
trust deed, 71–72
Truth in Lending Act, 68

usury, definition of, 72

ward, definition of, 50

About the Author

Roy M. Kodani, a partner in the firm Bays, Deaver, Hiatt, Kawachika, Lezak & Kodani, has practiced law in Hawaii since 1966. He specializes in international, real estate, corporate, and administrative law. He frequently serves as legal counsel to Pacific Rim companies and individuals.

Mr. Kodani has an A.B. degree from Lafayette College and earned his law degree from George Washington University Law School. After returning to Hawaii he served as a deputy attorney general for the state, during which time he was assigned to the Real Estate Commission and subsequently to the Department of Taxation. He has practiced before federal, state, and county administrative agencies and commissions as well as before federal and state courts.

From 1968 to 1969 he was secretary of the Board of Bar Examiners. He has been an Examiner of Titles of the Land Court since his appointment in 1973 and a licensed real estate broker since 1974. He is also a member of the panel of arbitrators of the American Arbitration Association and the First Circuit Arbitration program. He has been active with the Hawaii State Bar Association as a member of several committees and as an officer and director of the Young Lawyers Division.

[HAWAI] Production Notes

This book was designed by Roger Eggers. Composition and paging were done on the Quadex Composing System and typesetting on the Compugraphic 8400 by the design and production staff of University of Hawaii Press.

The text and display typeface is Galliard.

Offset presswork and binding were done by Malloy Lithographing, Inc. Text paper is Glatfelter Offset Vellum, basis 50.